Decorating with Paper & Paint

combining découpage & faux finish techniques

Decorating
with Paper & Paint

combining découpage & faux finish techniques

Rhonda Rainey

Sterling Publishing Co., Inc. New York
A Sterling/Chapelle Book

Chapelle Ltd.

Owner: Jo Packham

Design/layout Editor: Leslie Ridenour

Staff: Marie Barber, Ann Bear, Areta Bingham, Peggy Bowers, Kass Burchett, Rebecca Christensen, Holly Fuller, Marilyn Goff, Shirley Heslop, Holly Hollingsworth, Sherry Hoppe, Shawn Hsu, Susan Jorgensen, Pauline Locke, Barbara Milburn, Linda Orton, Karmen Quinney, Cindy Stoeckl

Acknowledgements: Several projects in this book were created with outstanding and innovative products developed by the following manufacturers: Plaid Enterprises Inc. of Norcross, Georgia, for acrylic paints and Royal Coat découpage medium; DecoArts Americana Paint of Stanford, Kentucky, for acrylic paints; Delta Technical Coatings of Whittier, California, for acrylic paints, glazes, and crackle medium; Havel Scissors of Cincinnati, Ohio, for découpage scissors; Fiskars of Wausau, Wisconsin, for craft and fabric scissors; and New Basics of Arvada, Colorado, for Wild Fiber papier maché. We would like to offer our sincere appreciation to these companies for the valuable support given in this ever changing industry of new ideas, concepts, designs, and products.

Library of Congress Cataloging-in-Publication Data

Rainey, Rhonda.
   Decorating with paper and paint : combining decoupage
& faux finish techniques / Rhonda Rainey
      p.   cm.
   "A Sterling/Chapelle book"
   Includes index.
   ISBN 0-8069-8171-7
   1. Découpage. I. Title.
TT870.R24   1998
745.54'6—dc21   98-3372
                          CIP

10 9 8 7 6 5 4 3 2 1

A Sterling/Chapelle Book

First paperback edition published in 1999 by
Sterling Publishing Company, Inc.
387 Park Avenue South, New York, N.Y. 10016
Produced by Chapelle Ltd.
P.O. Box 9252, Newgate Station, Ogden, Utah 84409
© 1998 by Chapelle Ltd.
Distributed in Canada by Sterling Publishing
% Canadian Manda Group, One Atlantic Avenue, Suite 105
Toronto, Ontario, Canada M6K 3E7
Distributed in Great Britain and Europe by Cassell PLC
Wellington House, 125 Strand, London WC2R 0BB, England
Distributed in Australia by Capricorn Link (Australia) Pty Ltd.
P.O. Box 6651, Baulkham Hills, Business Centre, NSW 2153, Australia
Printed in Hong Kong
All rights reserved

Sterling ISBN 0-8069-8171-7 Trade
           0-8069-8172-5 Paper

If you have any questions or comments or would like information about any specialty products featured in this book, please contact:

Chapelle Ltd., Inc.
P.O. Box 9252
Ogden, UT 84409

Phone: (801) 621-2777
FAX: (801) 621-2788

Table of Contents

About the Author

Rhonda Rainey is an artist of many interests and talents. She is an award-winning water colorist, designer, and published author.

Those associated with Rhonda find her to be thoughtful and innovative when it comes to pushing the boundaries of established crafting techniques. She approaches each new project with a fresh and spirited perspective.

An art educator for twenty years, Rhonda is currently working as a free-lance artist and designer. She is the mother of three grown children and a fun-loving grandmother. She resides in Idaho, where the rugged landscape and the quiet corners of nature provide subject matter for her work.

Introduction

This book presents several exciting ideas for personalizing and decorating your home by combining the relatively easy techniques of découpage and faux-finish. I call it "faux-page!"

Découpage is a decorative craft that has enjoyed popularity since the seventeenth century. Originally stemming from the French word *decouper*, meaning "to cut out," découpage is now accepted as the art of permanently decorating objects with a variety of cut or torn papers, fabrics, or natural materials.

Anything that can be cut or torn and pasted onto a surface, can be used to create découpage designs. With the advent of new glues and varnishes, and the availability of exotic and unusual papers, contemporary crafters have nearly endless possibilities when choosing materials to accent a special piece.

Faux-finish is the technique of transforming a plain, flat surface by artificially creating, with the use of acrylic paints, the texture and appearance of fine finishes, such as veined marble or burled wood.

I hope that this book will inspire and encourage you to try new materials and techniques and to let your imagination run wild!

Rhonda Rainey

Faux-page

Faux-page (fo-päzh) is a new yet easy technique that takes "added elements" and creatively combines these with the traditional methods and materials (paint, paper, and découpage medium) used in both faux-finishing and découpage techniques, giving today's crafter unlimited potential for creating new and unusual patterns, textures, and colors.

Faux finishing techniques, previously sometimes complicated and reserved for wood and walls, have been simplified, adapted, and added to everyday images, objects, and materials, as well as the simple art of découpage for this new faux-page paper/paint application. With this new method there is little required in the way of drawing or painting skills, so the technique is truly non-threatening. For example, a flower, made up of petals, leaves, and a stem, when combined with paint and paper, can become a splash of colors—blues, greens, and lavenders—as well as a study in texture. Nearly unrecognizable now as a flower, another dimension has been added to the overall color and texture of the faux-finished découpage design surface through this one small added element.

Faux-page is the newest, simplest, and most creative way of decorating anything—from walls and furniture to glass vases and mirrors. It is a technique that offers such a variety of effects that it will become as recognizable as the traditional techniques of faux-finishing and découpage.

Paper, Supplies, & Tools

Paper
One of the great pleasures of this craft is the stunning variety of papers now available. Because it is such an integral part of everyday life, only recently has paper come into its own as an expressive and versatile art medium.

The majority of papers used in this book are available at craft stores, office supply stores, stationery shops, and even the local supermarket—gift wrap in the greeting card section and butcher paper at the meat counter. The appearance of even the most ordinary papers can be altered by using simple techniques to change their color, texture, finish, and surface. All it requires to master these techniques is a willingness to try something new, an openness to a variety of possibilities, and a little practice.

For those who wish to explore the world of handmade and exotic imported papers, a list of suppliers is provided on page 127. Catalogs and paper samples are often available from these suppliers that allow the buyer to preview these papers before purchasing them. Be certain to call or write for availability and cost as some papers can be expensive.

Découpage Medium
All projects in this book were completed using découpage medium as both the binder and the final finish. It is used to adhere paper, fabric, and other porous materials. It can be used as a

sealer for paper, prints, acrylic paints, stains, and wood. It is available in a gloss, matte or antique finish. It is quick drying, dries clear, and can be sanded to a smooth finish.

Paint

Acrylic paints and mediums were chosen largely for their versatility in completing the faux finishes in this book. Acrylics are inexpensive, readily available, found in a wide range of colors and finishes, and fast drying. When diluted with water, acrylics can also be used for watercolor techniques. Watercolors and waterbase inks tend to lift and run when the découpage medium is applied and, therefore, are not suitable for these projects.

Paintbrushes

Good results can be obtained with only a few paintbrushes. A synthetic 1" flat watercolor paintbrush is the most versatile. This type of paintbrush is much less likely to lose its bristles. It is best to use a different paintbrush for the découpage medium than those used for painting. Otherwise, small flecks of paint can taint the medium.

A #2 round watercolor paintbrush is ideal for detailing, painting in small areas, and touch ups. The #8 round watercolor paintbrush is used for watercolor-type painting on the papers that will later be torn or cut and adhered as part of the design. A #2 script liner paintbrush has a very thin long tip. It is ideal for the Faux Tortoise Shell technique found on pages 102 and 104–105. The 1" China bristle sash paintbrush is available at all paint and hardware stores. The bristles are longer and more coarse than the artist's paintbrushes. The China bristle sash paintbrush is inexpensive and is an asset to any crafter's toolbox. The long coarse bristles are perfect for painting faux crackle finish on découpage papers.

Paint Palettes & Mixing Containers

When mixing small amounts of paint, a disposable palette is handy. However, when mixing larger amounts of paint or diluting découpage medium with water, several wide-mouth, heavy plastic cups are a necessity.

Cleaning Paintbrushes & Work Material

To clean découpage medium and acrylic paint from paintbrushes, a good washing with isopropyl/ethyl alcohol is recommended. Clean the paintbrushes thoroughly and then wash again with soap and warm—not hot—water. Shape bristles and lay flat to dry.

Craft Tips

Craft tips are tools used to create extremely fine line work with acrylic paint, fabric paint, and slower setting adhesives. These tips are usually available in sets that contain extension caps, bottles, and metal tips.

Sponges

Several projects call for paint to be applied with a sponge. To achieve the particular looks shown, a kitchen/house-hold sponge that is at least 3" thick and has fairly large pores is best. A large sponge should be cut into smaller, workable pieces with a pair of craft scissors.

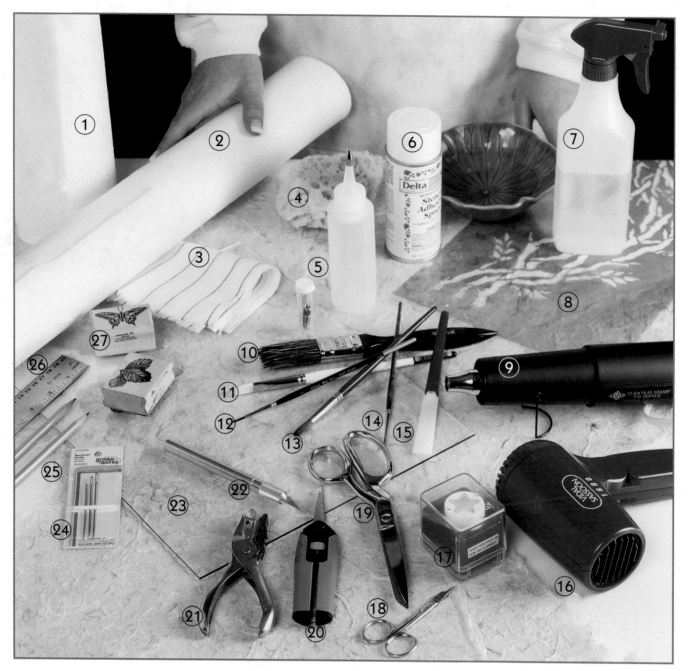

General Tools

1. Paper towels
2. Butcher paper
3. Lint-free cloth
4. Sponge
5. Fine-point craft tip set
6. Stencil adhesive
7. Spray bottle filled with water
8. Precut stencil
9. Heat tool

10. China bristle sash paintbrush
11. 1" flat watercolor paintbrush
12. #2 round watercolor paintbrush
13. #8 round watercolor paintbrush
14. #2 script liner paintbrush
15. Stylus
16. Blow dryer
17. Large decorative paper punch
18. Découpage scissors

19. Fabric scissors
20. Craft scissors
21. Small decorative paper punch
22. Craft knife
23. Glass for cutting
24. Crewel needles
25. Pencils
26. Straight-edge metal ruler
27. Rubber stamps

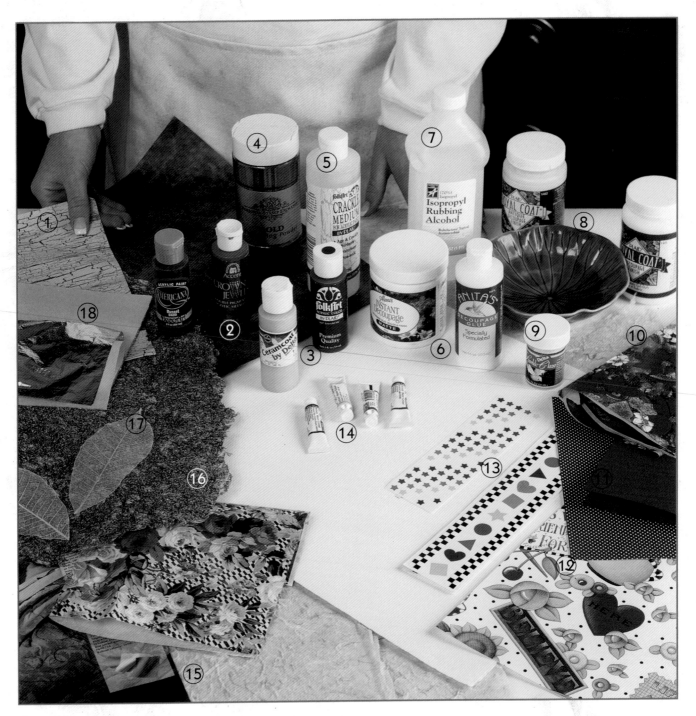

General Materials

1. Faux hand-painted papers
2. Pearlized glaze acrylic paint
3. Acrylic paint
4. Embossing powder
5. Crackle medium
6. Découpage medium

7. Isopropyl alcohol
8. Container of clean water
9. Glitter glaze
10. Patterned gift wrap
11. Colored cardstock
12. Decorative paper/stationery

13. Stickers
14. Watercolor paints
15. Magazine pages
16. Papier maché lace
17. Natural veined leaves
18. Gold leafing

Specialty Papers

1. Heavy-weight Unryu paper
2. Japanese lace paper
3. Marbleized paper
4. Unryu tissue paper
5. Colored Unryu tissue paper
6. Medium-weight Japanese Mulberry paper
7. Gold tissue paper
8. Gold foil paper
9. Coarse handmade paper
10. Handmade lace paper
11. Marbleized gift wrap

General Techniques

Preparing Surfaces

Any object that has a properly prepared surface can be used with this new technique. The surface must be clean and smooth. All joints in a piece of furniture must be tightened and secure. Minor repairs, such as filling gouges, cracks, and holes with spackling compound or water putty, should be made to furniture. If the hole is large, it should be coated with glue first to help the filler remain in its place. Some types of water-base wood fillers shrink and will require more than one layer to bring them up to the surface. Allow each layer to dry thoroughly. When the last layer is dry, gently sand the surface, working with the grain of the wood. After sanding, rub well, using a tack cloth. Apply a coat of découpage medium over the surface to seal it. Then apply acrylic paint or cover with paper to create the background as directed in individual project instructions.

Always read the product labels and follow the manufacturer's instructions for the materials in use. It is also helpful to keep hands clean and glue-free. Stubborn découpage medium can be removed with isopropyl alcohol.

Shaping Papers

Although the original meaning of the word *découpage* means "to cut," the majority of the projects in this book use a torn paper technique. Tearing produces a rough, feathery edge except when a ruler is used to yield a tear that is more controlled. Because the paper's inner fibers become visible and the edges are random, this technique causes a spontaneous feeling to be associated with the design of the project.

There are several ways to tear paper to produce interesting edges. Papers have a grain and a surface texture that affect the outcome of the tear. Woven papers have a smooth, harder finish; while laid papers have a slightly ribbed surface. If a paper is torn along ("with") the grain, the resulting tear will follow a fairly straight line and will require little effort. Tearing across the grain produces a ragged edge that can only be torn an inch or so at a time.

Printed, painted, and coated papers can be torn two ways to produce different edges (fig. 1). If the paper is torn toward the body, the fibers on the left side of the tear will be exposed. These will generally show white. The paper at the right side of the tear will show the surface color and texture to the very edge of the tear. If the paper is torn away from the body, the opposite effect is produced.

Colored paper that is dyed through will not produce a white edge when torn. These papers can be important elements when a subtle, blended effect is desired for the project.

The easiest and most successful way to tear and shape a soft-finish paper (Japanese and Indian papers) is to wet a #2 round watercolor paintbrush with water and "draw" the shape with the wet paintbrush. Using a large crewel needle with a blunt tip, carefully pull the dry paper away from the wet edge (fig. 2). Lift the shape and set aside.

(fig. 1)   Tearing printed, painted, or coated papers leaves the white inner fibers exposed to view. Tearing paper toward the body will expose the fibers on the left edge, while tearing away from the body will expose the fibers on the right edge.

(fig. 2)   Papers that have a soft finish or are heavily fibered can be more easily torn by first wetting the desired shape, using a small paintbrush and clean water. Then, using a needle, tear along damp edge and lift away desired shape.

To make very delicate and detailed cuts, the best tool to use is a craft knife. Cut on glass or self-healing cutting mat to protect work surfaces. When doing a great deal of work with a craft knife, blades must be replaced frequently as they tend to dull quickly.

Sharp scissors are a necessity for découpage crafting. Projects require a small pair of pointed manicure-type *découpage scissors* for cutting detail, a pair of larger *craft scissors* for cutting larger and heavier pieces of paper and materials, and a pair of *fabric scissors* for achieving clean fabric edges. *All cutting tools should be kept out of reach of children!*

Applying Découpage Medium

It is best to practice with any découpage medium to make certain the materials being used will adhere and remain in place. In general, the heavier the paper (cardstock, wallpaper, watercolor paper), the thicker the medium must be.

Many water-base mediums tend to lose their "tack" as they are diluted with water. However, many products, unless diluted, are much too heavy for fine- and light-weight papers. It is best to experiment with different amounts of water.

When diluting, pour a small amount (approximately 4 oz.) of the medium into a plastic cup. Mix in a few drops of clean water and stir. Continue adding water and stirring until desired consistency is achieved.

Apply découpage medium to the surface of the project. Lay the papers into the wet medium. This technique makes the handling of light- to medium-weight papers much easier. When handling heavier papers, a coat of medium on the back of the paper, as well as on the project surface, will help keep everything in its place. Brush découpage medium over laid paper from the center outward to protect and seal edges (fig. 3).

To protect against dirt, dust, and stains, surfaces must be sealed. All projects should receive at least five to seven coats of découpage medium to finish. Water-base acrylic varnish can also be used to avoid any yellowing that may come with age. If the finished project is placed where there will be bright or direct sunlight, applying a water-base exterior varnish that is U-V light and weather resistant is also recommended.

Dry-brush Technique

Dry-brush is a painting technique which allows the undercolor or undertone to show through a thinly applied top layer of paint (fig. 4). No water is used in dry-brushing. Dab a flat paintbrush into thicker paint and then blot on a paper towel. Drag the loaded paintbrush across the painting surface. The amount of paint used, the angle of the paintbrush, and the speed of the stroke will determine the final look. It is best to practice this technique before working on the project.

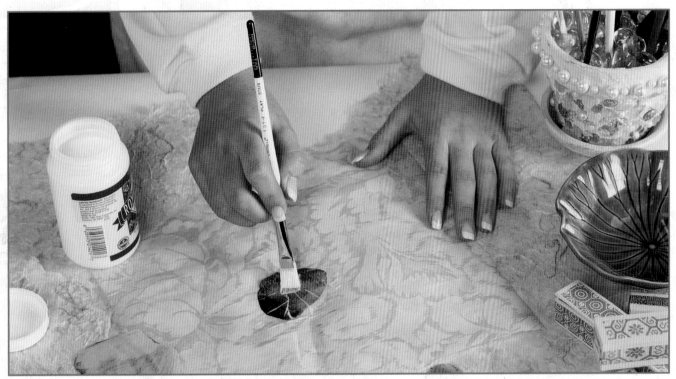

(fig. 3) Lay the shape on the project surface and gently brush découpage medium from the center outward to protect and seal edges. Brushing against the edge can lift the shape and result in unwanted ridges.

(fig. 4) Dry-brushing provides an antiqued look—giving the appearance of skipped-over or missed areas on the surface. Dab a flat paintbrush in paint and blot on a paper towel. Brush a thin, broken layer of paint lightly across project surface.

Papier Appliqué

Papier Appliqué

Materials
Acrylic paints: white; metallic gold
Découpage medium
Gift wrap: patterned
Japanese lace paper
Tissue paper: white, light-weight

General Supplies & Tools
Craft tip set: fine-point
Découpage scissors
Paintbrushes: 1" flat watercolor (2);
  #2 round watercolor

Instructions
1. Refer to Preparing Surfaces on page 8. Prepare project surface.

2. Using a flat paintbrush, paint project surface with white paint.

3. Cut patterned designs from gift wrap.

4. Using another flat paintbrush, apply découpage medium onto project surface, working small areas at a time. Press gift wrap designs into découpage medium, overlapping designs as desired. Leave several small and large areas of white background exposed. Let dry, then brush with another coat of découpage medium.

5. Tear tissue paper into random shapes and sizes suitable to project. Brush découpage medium onto some of the gift wrap designs and lay tissue over the designs. Brush découpage medium onto tissue areas and lay another gift wrap design over the tissue.

6. Tear lace paper into random shapes and sizes. Brush découpage medium onto desired areas of surface and adhere lace paper pieces to surface (fig. 1). Brush découpage medium onto lace paper pieces and lay more gift wrap designs over lace paper pieces. Let dry.

7. Following manufacturer's instructions for use of craft tip set, outline patterned designs with metallic gold paint (fig. 2). Let dry.

8. Using round paintbrush, fill in small areas of white background with metallic gold paint. Let dry.

9. Using flat paintbrush, apply several coats of découpage medium over papered surface, allowing medium to dry between each coat.

Materials: Patterned gift wrap, Japanese lace paper, tissue paper, découpage medium, and acrylic paint.

(fig. 1)   Brush surface with découpage medium. Press lace paper into medium, adhering to surface.

(fig. 2)   Using craft tip set, outline patterned designs on gift wrap with metallic gold paint.

Natural Leaf Prints

Natural Leaf Prints

Materials
Acrylic paints: metallic gold;
  additional colors of choice
Butcher paper: white
Découpage medium
Fresh leaves
Japanese Bekko lace paper
Japanese Mulberry paper: two shades

General Supplies & Tools
Crewel needle: large
Disposable paint palette
Paintbrushes: 1" flat watercolor (2)
Paper towels

Instructions
1. Refer to Preparing Surfaces on page 8. Prepare project surface.

2. For each color of paint, except gold, mix one part paint with five parts water on palette. Mix well.

3. Using a flat paintbrush, brush butcher paper with clean water until surface glistens.

4. Drag paintbrush across paper towels to remove excess moisture, then dip into paint mixture to pick up color. Touch paintbrush and paint to wet surface at top edge of paper (fig. 1). Pull paint from top to bottom of page. The wetter the paper, the softer and more feathery the brush strokes will appear. If the paper dries too quickly, rinse paintbrush and add more clean water to paper surface and repeat process. Let dry.

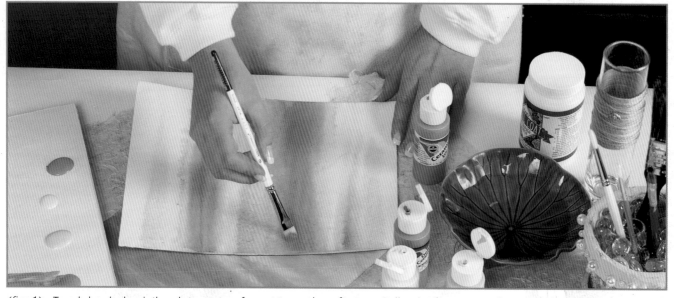

(fig. 1) Touch loaded paintbrush to wet surface at top edge of paper. Pull paint from top to bottom of page, allowing colors to blend and mix. The more water that is used, the softer the edges will appear.

5. Rinse leaves in clean water. Pat leaf dry with paper towels. Place leaf, vein side up, on work surface and lightly brush with full-strength color of paint. Highlight desired areas with metallic gold paint (fig. 2).

(fig. 2)   Place leaf, vein side up, on work surface and lightly brush with full-strength acrylic paint. Highlight desired areas with metallic gold paint.

6. Tear pieces of Mulberry paper slightly larger than leaf. Place paper over leaf and gently press, using a pad of paper towels to make an imprint (fig. 3). Carefully separate leaf and paper. Dry imprint.

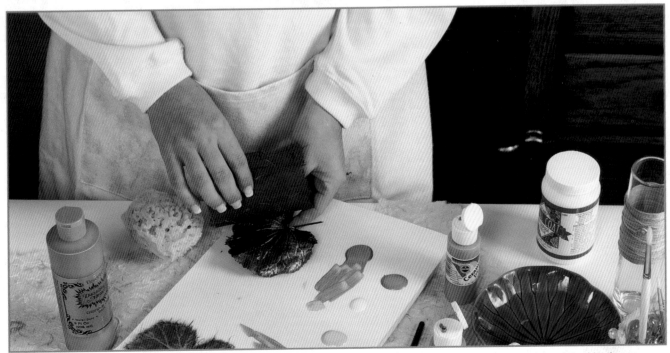

(fig. 3)   Place leaf on a hard surface and make an imprint by gently pressing torn Mulberry paper onto painted leaf.

7. Using paintbrush, outline imprinted leaf with clean water. Using crewel needle, gently pull excess paper away from printed leaf, leaving a feathery edge. Repeat Steps 5–7 for desired number of leaves.

8. Tear Bekko paper and painted paper from Step 4 into random shapes and sizes suitable to project.

9. Using another flat paintbrush, apply découpage medium onto project surface, working small areas at a time. Press painted paper shapes into découpage medium, then brush a coat of medium over paper shapes. Let dry. Repeat process to adhere leaves, then to adhere Bekko paper shapes.

10. Brush several coats of découpage medium over papered surface, allowing medium to dry between each coat.

Foliage

Materials
Acrylic paints: metallic gold; dark color; deep color; light color
Crackle medium
Découpage medium
Dried leaves
Leafing: gold and copper

General Supplies & Tools
Lint-free cloth
Paintbrushes: 1" flat watercolor (2); 1" China bristle sash
Small cup
Small sponge

Instructions
1. Refer to Preparing Surfaces on page 8. Prepare project surface.

2. Using a flat paintbrush, brush a thin coat of découpage medium onto project surface. Let dry.

3. Using another flat paintbrush, apply dark color of paint to project surface.

Materials: Acrylic paints, crackle medium, découpage medium, dried leaves, and gold and copper leafing.

4. Following manufacturer's instructions, brush a generous coat of crackle medium onto project surface. Thoroughly rinse paintbrush.

5. Using sash paintbrush, apply light color of paint over crackle medium.

6. Squeeze 1–2 drops deep color of paint into small cup and mix with one tablespoon water. Brush diluted paint over project surface. Gently wipe with cloth or slightly damp sponge for an antique appearance (fig. 1).

7. Using a flat paintbrush, apply a coat of découpage medium to seal project.

8. Using sponge, apply deep color of paint onto front of veined leaves. Work paint with sponge so open areas are not filled in and leaves remain lacy.

9. Using a flat paintbrush, brush backs of leaves with découpage medium and adhere them to project surface, making certain to smooth any air bubbles or loose edges.

10. Using another flat paintbrush, dry-brush metallic gold paint over textured surface of leaves, focusing on the heavier veins, and onto desired areas of project base.

11. Following manufacturer's instructions, apply gold and copper leafing in a random pattern over leaves and project base.

(fig. 1)   After surface has been brushed with dark paint, lift excess, using a cloth or slightly damp sponge to create an antique appearance.

Foliage

Faux Marble

Faux Marble

Materials
Acrylic paints: metallic; colors of
  choice
Découpage medium
Handwritten letters
Magazine photos
Paper scraps
Postcards
Stamped and postmarked envelopes
Tissue papers: patterned with light,
  medium, and dark areas; patterned
  with very light shadows

General Supplies & Tools
Craft scissors
Disposable paint palette
Paintbrushes: 1" flat watercolor
Rubber stamps: postage-themed

Instructions
1. Refer to Preparing Surfaces on page
8. Prepare project surface.

2. Cut out or tear desired images from
postcards, magazines, envelopes, and
letters in random shapes and sizes
suitable for project. Tear tissue papers
into small pieces.

3. Spread a thin layer of color of paint
onto palette to use as ink for stamps.
Mix colors if desired. Ink stamps in paint
and stamp onto paper scraps. Cut from
paper.

4. Dilute découpage medium with water
to a light, creamy consistency. Brush
medium onto project surface, working
small areas at a time. Press dark tissue
paper pieces into medium. Smooth with
paintbrush, making certain all paper
edges are sealed. Repeat process, layering light over dark tissue paper pieces.

5. Arrange paper and stamped images
as desired on surface. Brush surface
with découpage medium and press
images into medium. Brush several
coats of découpage medium over
papered surface, allowing medium to
dry between each coat.

6. Repeat Step 3 (do not cut out), stamp-
ing directly onto project surface. Let dry.

7. Brush several more coats of
découpage medium over papered
surface.

Materials: Patterned tissue papers, letters, postcards, paper
scraps, and découpage medium.

Patterned Napkins

Materials
Acrylic paint: metallic gold
Découpage medium
Gift wraps: coordinating patterned;
  one additional high-contrast patterned
Japanese lace paper
Paper napkin: patterned
Tissue paper: metallic or pearlized

General Supplies & Tools
Blow dryer
Découpage scissors
Paintbrushes: 1" flat watercolor
Small sponge

Instructions
1. Refer to Preparing Surfaces on page 8. Prepare project surface.

2. Tear or cut napkin into random shapes and sizes suitable to project.

3. Brush découpage medium onto project surface, working small areas at a time. Using paintbrush, gently press napkin shapes into découpage medium. Smooth all wrinkles. Let dry.

4. Tear high-contrast gift wrap and tissue paper into small, postage stamp-sized pieces. Following process in Step 3, adhere paper pieces to project surface, overlapping torn edges.

5. Tear lace paper into small pieces. Brush découpage medium onto desired areas of papered surface and adhere lace paper pieces to surface. Let dry, then brush on another coat of découpage medium.

6. Cut out large patterned designs from gift wrap. Repeat process in Step 4, making certain all edges are sealed. Adhere more lace paper pieces over large designs, if desired.

7. When overall design is satisfactory, brush several coats of découpage medium over surface, allowing medium to dry between each coat. Use a blow dryer to accelerate drying.

8. Dip damp sponge into metallic gold paint and randomly sponge-paint pattern over surface. Let dry, then brush three or four more coats of découpage medium onto surface.

Materials: Patterned contrasting gift wraps, Japanese lace paper, patterned paper napkins, and metallic tissue paper.

Patterned Napkins

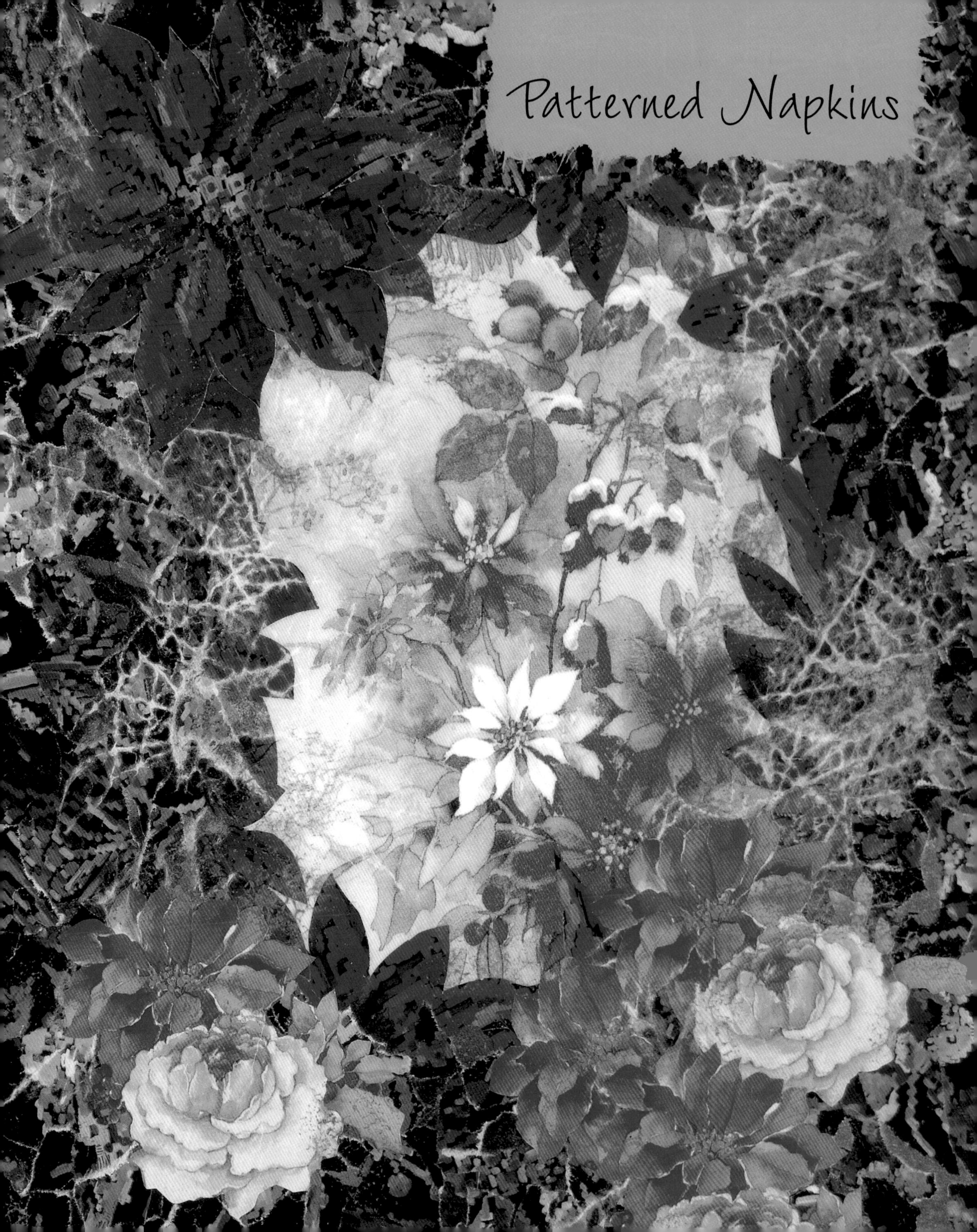

Glazing Paper

Glazing Paper

Materials
Acrylic paints: metallic gold; dark shade; light shade
Butcher paper with duplex surface (one side wax-coated; one side uncoated)
Crackle medium
Découpage medium: satin
Gift wrap: patterned
Japanese Mulberry paper: heavy-weight
Tissue paper: metallic gold

General Supplies & Tools
Découpage scissors
Paintbrushes: 1" flat watercolor (2); 1" China bristle sash
Small sponge

Instructions
1. Refer to Preparing Surfaces on page 8. Prepare project surface.

2. Following manufacturer's instructions and using sash paintbrush, apply colors of paint and crackle medium to coated side of butcher paper. Repeat process, reversing colors, on another sheet of butcher paper. Set paper aside to dry.

3. Dilute one drop dark color of paint with one tablespoon water. Using a flat paintbrush, brush onto tissue paper. When dry, tear tissue into small pieces.

4. Dip paintbrush into clean water and draw free-form shapes on Mulberry paper. Gently tear shapes from paper on dampened lines. Torn edges will have a feathered appearance.

5. Cut patterned designs from gift wrap.

6. Tear crackled butcher paper into shapes and sizes suitable for project.

7. Using another flat paintbrush, apply découpage medium onto project surface, working small areas at a time. Using damp sponge and clean water, moisten back of crackled butcher papers. Immediately adhere papers to area where medium has been applied. Using sponge to smooth, gently press papers. Papers may be overlapped and direction of crackle changed. Repeat process for Mulberry paper shapes, gift wrap designs, and tissue pieces.

8. Brush several coats of découpage medium over papered surface, allowing medium to dry between each coat.

9. Mix 2–3 drops of metallic gold paint with one tablespoon découpage medium. Using a flat paintbrush, randomly dry-brush paint over surface. Let dry. Apply several more coats of découpage medium.

Materials: Patterned gift wrap, Japanese Mulberry paper, gold tissue paper, acrylic paints, and découpage medium.

Shapes & Edges

Materials
Acrylic paints: metallics (2); dark shade; medium shade; light shade
Butcher paper
Découpage medium
Japanese Unryu paper: sheer
Veined fossil leaves: 2

General Supplies & Tools
Disposable paint palette
Paintbrushes: 1" flat watercolor (2)
Plastic cup
Small sponge
Stencil adhesive
Stencils: two large leaf patterns

Instructions
1. Refer to Preparing Surfaces on page 8. Prepare project surface.

Materials: Acrylic paints, découpage medium, stencils, Unryu paper, and veined fossil leaves.

2. Squeeze three colors of paint onto palette. Using damp sponge, apply paint, one color over another, onto butcher paper (fig. 1). Let dry. Thoroughly wash sponge.

(fig. 1) Working from dark to light, alternately sponge three different paint colors on butcher paper. Allow paint to dry between layers.

3. Tear sponged paper and Unryu paper into random shapes and sizes suitable to project.

4. Using a flat paintbrush, apply découpage medium onto project surface. Press sponged paper pieces into medium and brush to smooth and flatten. Let dry.

5. Dilute two parts découpage medium with one part water in plastic cup. Brush thinned medium onto project surface. Press Unryu paper pieces into medium.

6. Squeeze small amount of three colors of paint onto palette. Spray back of stencils with stencil adhesive. Using sponge, apply dark color within one leaf stencil pattern to project (fig. 2). Partially sponge, moving stencil to vary leaf length. Let dry. Wash sponge and repeat process with medium color and second leaf stencil (fig. 3). Repeat process with light color and first leaf stencil. Let dry. Using a flat paintbrush, apply one coat of découpage medium over project surface.

7. Using another flat paintbrush, brush veined leaves with metallic colors of paint. Clean paintbrush with soap and water.

8. Using a flat paintbrush, apply découpage medium onto desired areas for leaves. Gently press one leaf into medium and brush edges to seal (fig. 4). Tear second leaf into small pieces and press into medium.

9. Brush several coats of découpage medium over surface, allowing medium to dry between each coat.

(fig. 2)   Sponge darkest paint color within stencil onto surface for first layer of pattern. Let dry and then remove stencil to avoid smearing paint.

(fig. 3) Sponge medium paint color within a second stencil onto surface for first layer of pattern. Let dry and then remove stencil from surface.

(fig. 4) Apply découpage medium to project surface. Determine placement of leaf and press leaf into wet medium. Gently brush leaf from center to outside edges to adhere.

Shapes & Edges

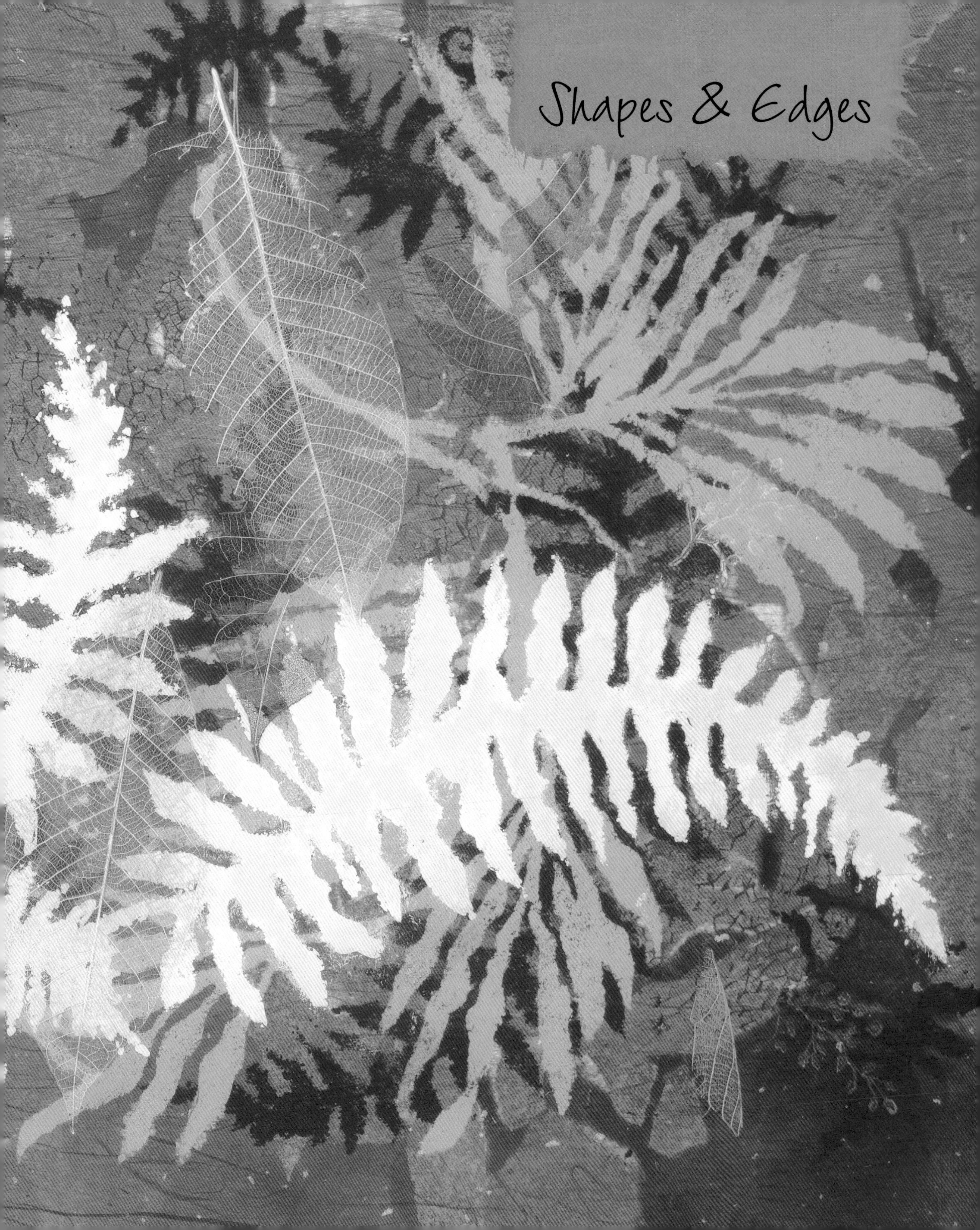

Foil Inlay

Foil Inlay

Materials
Acrylic paints: metallics; one dark
  color of choice
Butcher paper: white
Cardstock paper: 80 or 90 lb.
Découpage medium

General Supplies & Tools
Craft knife with #11 blade
Cutting surface: glass or cutting mat
Disposable paint palette
Paintbrushes: 1" flat watercolor (2);
  #2 round watercolor
Small sponge
Stencil adhesive
Stencils: of choice

Instructions
1. Refer to Preparing Surfaces on page 8. Prepare project surface.

2. Squeeze a small amount of each metallic color of paint onto palette. Using a flat paintbrush and damp sponge, apply paints to cardstock paper to achieve an uneven, mottled effect (fig. 1). Let dry. Apply more color in various areas as desired. Repeat process on butcher paper, working for a lighter and brighter effect.

3. Spray back of stencil with stencil adhesive and adhere to painted cardstock paper. Using damp sponge, apply dark color of paint within stencil pattern to paper. Using sponge, add subtle texture with metallic colors. Let dry, then remove stencil.

4. Place stenciled design on cutting surface. Using craft knife, cut out desired areas (fig. 2).

5. Using round paintbrush and a metallic color of paint, paint detail lines at edges of stenciled design. Let dry.

6. Using another flat paintbrush, apply découpage medium onto painted butcher paper. Press stenciled design into medium to complete inlay. Let dry. Brush découpage medium onto project surface and press paper inlay into medium. Let dry.

7. Brush several coats of découpage medium over papered surface, allowing medium to dry between each coat.

Materials: Butcher paper, colored cardstock, acrylic paints, stencil, craft knife, and paintbrushes.

(fig. 1) Apply paints to cardstock paper to achieve an uneven, mottled effect.

(fig. 2) Place stenciled design on cutting surface. Using craft knife, cut out desired areas of stenciled design. A small overcut will allow shapes to come free.

Bits & Pieces

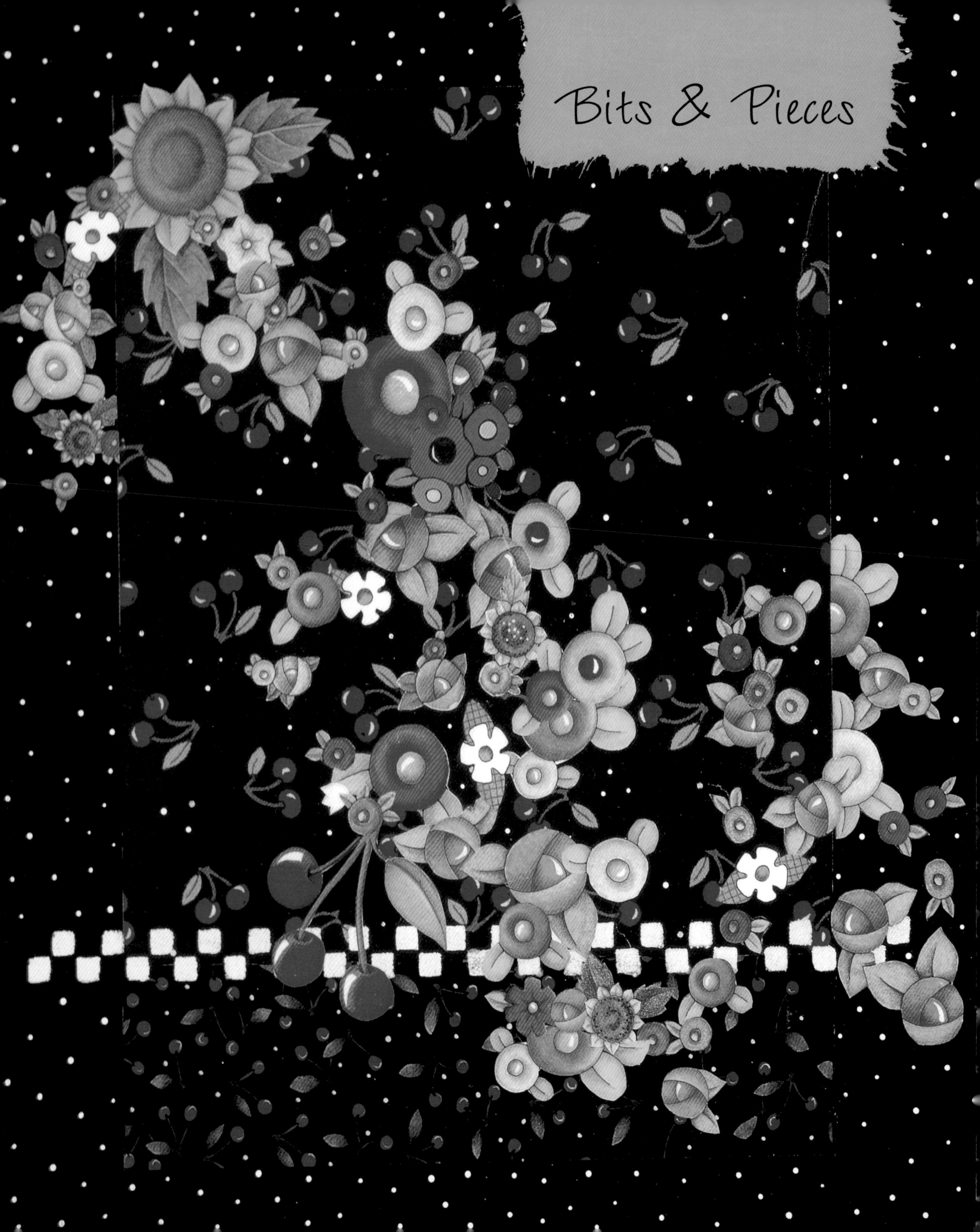

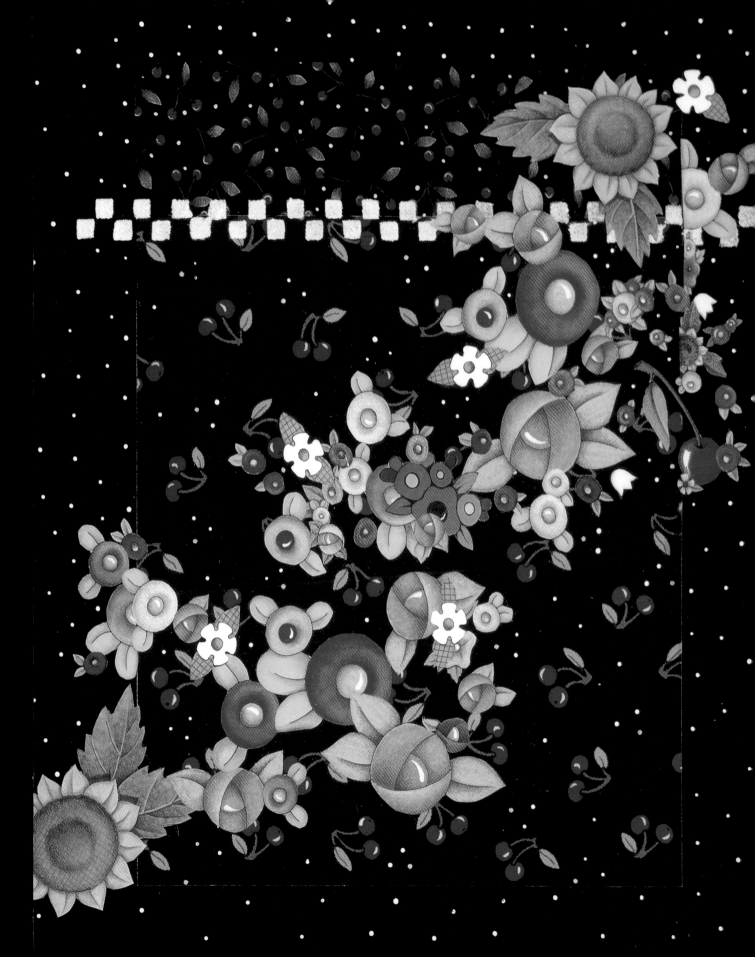

Bits & Pieces

Materials
Acrylic paints: two contrasting colors of choice
Decorative stationery and envelopes
Découpage medium
Stickers

General Supplies & Tools
Découpage scissors
Paintbrushes: 1" flat watercolor (2)
Small sponge
Stencil: ¼" checkered
Stencil adhesive
Stylus

Instructions
1. Refer to Preparing Surfaces on page 8. Prepare project surface.

2. Using a flat paintbrush, apply two coats of color of paint onto project. Let dry.

3. Dilute two parts découpage medium with one part water. Using another flat paintbrush, apply a generous coat of diluted medium onto painted areas of project. Let dry.

4. Cut motifs from decorative stationery and envelopes.

5. Brush découpage medium over project surface, working small areas at a time. Press motifs into medium, smoothing as needed (fig. 1). Motifs may be clustered, overlapped, or spread out as desired. Let dry.

6. Brush diluted medium over papered surface. Let dry.

7. Adhere stickers to project surface as desired.

8. Spray back of stencil with stencil adhesive and adhere to desired area. Using sponge, apply second color of paint within stencil pattern.

9. Dip stylus into paint and randomly create a polka dot pattern on surface (fig. 2).

10. Using a flat paintbrush, apply several coats of full-strength découpage medium over papered surface, allowing medium to dry between each coat.

Materials: Decorative stationery, stickers, acrylic paints, découpage medium, découpage scissors, and paintbrushes.

(fig. 1)   Cluster cut-out motifs and press into découpaged surface.

(fig. 2)   Dip stylus into paint and randomly create a polka dot pattern on painted surface.

Paper Weaving

Paper Weaving

Materials
Decorative papers: assorted medium- to heavy-weight
Découpage medium
Japanese Unryu paper: sheer
Paper for base: white or color of choice

General Supplies & Tools
Craft knife with #11 blade
Craft scissors
Cutting surface: glass or cutting mat
Metal-edge ruler
Paintbrushes: 1" flat watercolor
Paper adhesive
Pencil

Instructions
1. Refer to Preparing Surfaces on page 8. Prepare project surface.

2. Using a craft knife and ruler, cut decorative papers into strips of desired widths and lengths on cutting surface.

3. Using paper adhesive, tack vertical strips along top edge of base paper (fig. 1).

4. Choose strips for horizontal placement and weave into place. Adhere each end of woven horizontal strips to first and last vertical strips.

5. Brush découpage medium onto woven surface. Press Unryu paper into medium (fig. 2). Brush gently to secure, adding medium as needed. Let dry.

6. Brush several coats of découpage medium onto woven surface, allowing medium to dry between each coat.

7. Turn paper over and peel off loose areas of base paper (fig. 3). Brush backside of woven paper with découpage medium to seal.

8. Using craft scissors, cut woven paper into desired shapes and sizes or use entire sheet for project.

(fig. 1) With vertical strips tacked along top edge of base paper, weave horizontal strips, tacking ends to first and last vertical strips.

(fig. 2)   Press Unryu paper onto surface that has been coated with découpage medium.

(fig. 3)   Peel base paper away from woven paper.

Faux Leather

Materials
Découpage medium
Paper of choice: brown, heavy-weight

General Supplies & Tools
Cookie pan
Paintbrushes: 1" flat watercolor

Instructions
1. Refer to Preparing Surfaces on page 8. Prepare project surface.

2. Tear paper into random shapes and sizes suitable to project. Soak paper pieces in warm water for 2–3 minutes. Remove from water and squeeze to remove excess moisture. Carefully flatten damp papers on cookie pan.

3. Brush découpage medium onto a small area of project surface. Brush medium onto a piece of paper and press paper onto surface. Brush from center of paper to outside edges to smooth. Make certain paper is flat to the surface and all edges are sealed. Continue process, overlapping paper pieces, until surface is covered. Allow surface to thoroughly dry.

4. Brush several coats of découpage medium over papered surface, allowing medium to dry between each coat.

If technique is to be used on a floor as in *Brown Paper Chic* on page 114, follow these steps:

Materials
Paper: brown, heavy-weight
Polyurethane varnish: clear, quick-dry waterbase

General Supplies & Tools
Container: wide-mouth plastic gallon with lid
Cookie pan
Craft glue
Paint pan
Paintbrushes: 4" natural bristle varnish (2)

Instructions
1. Prepare floor by making certain all seams and holes are filled and nails are counter-sunk. Sand, vacuum, then damp-mop.

2. Dilute one part glue with two parts water in container. Mix well. Pour into paint pan.

3. Follow Steps 3–4 above, substituting diluted glue, varnish paintbrushes, and varnish. Following manufacturer's instructions, apply five coats of varnish to floor to seal.

Pictures for Design

Materials
Colored craft paper
Découpage medium
Gift wrap: themed
Glitter glaze
Japanese Unryu paper: sheer
Magazine pages: assorted colors and
    textures
Stickers

General Supplies & Tools
Craft scissors
Decorative paper punches: small, large
Paintbrushes: 1" flat watercolor

Instructions

1. Refer to Preparing Surfaces on page 8. Prepare project surface.

2. Tear magazine pages with desired colors and textures into random shapes and sizes suitable to project. Tear Unryu paper into random shapes and sizes.

3. Punch various shapes from craft paper and cut motifs from gift wrap.

4. Brush découpage medium onto project surface, working small areas at a time. Press magazine pieces into medium. Firmly brush to flatten and seal edges. Continue process until surface is covered with torn papers. Let dry, then brush papered surface with découpage medium. Let dry.

5. Brush découpage medium onto surface. Press punched shapes and stickers into medium. Let dry. Brush medium onto surface. Press pieces of Unryu paper into medium. Let dry.

6. Brush glitter glaze over desired areas.

7. Brush several coats of découpage medium over papered surfaces, allowing medium to dry between each coat.

Materials: Themed gift wrap, magazine pages, Japanese Unryu paper, decorative paper punches, and découpage medium.

Pictures for Design

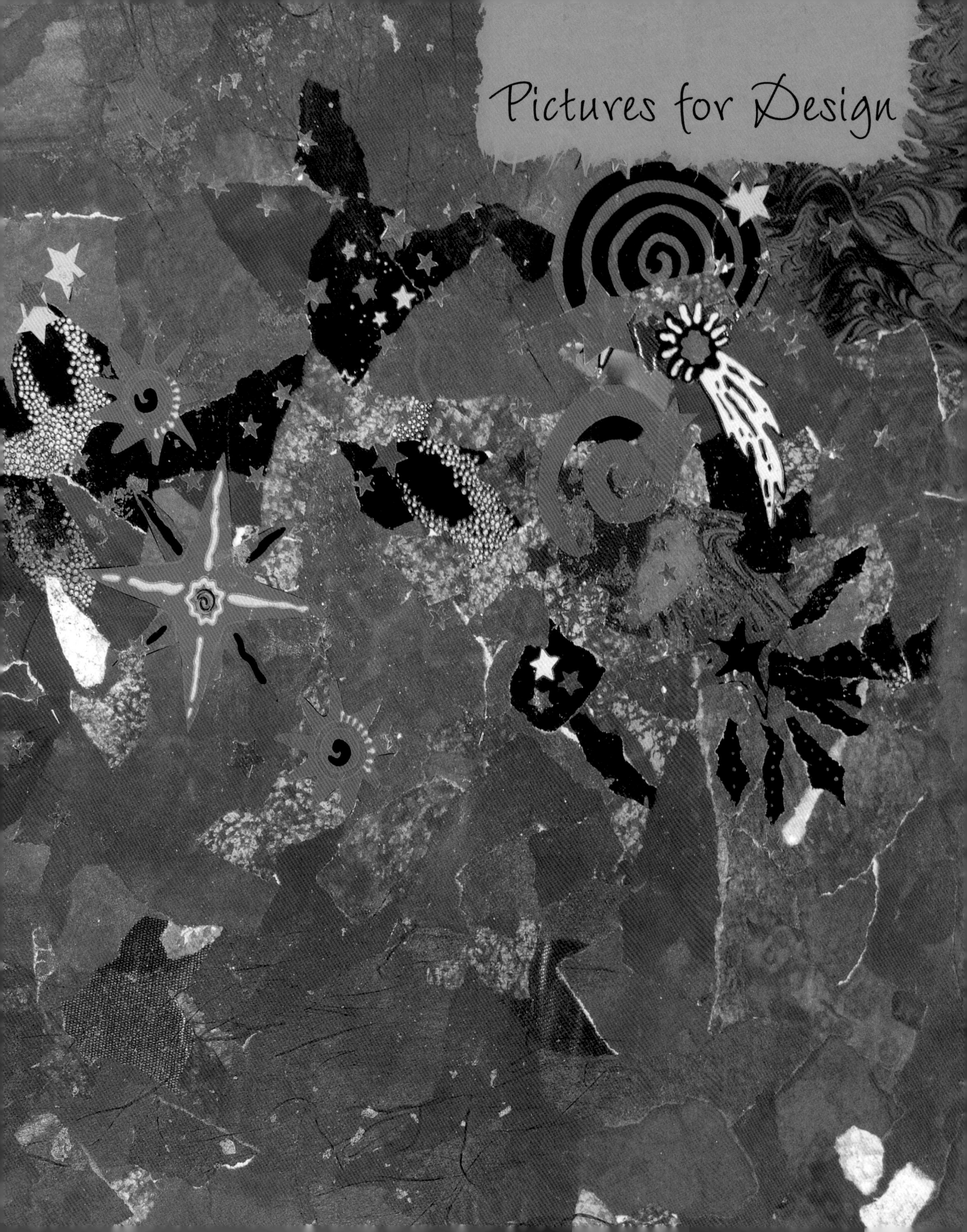

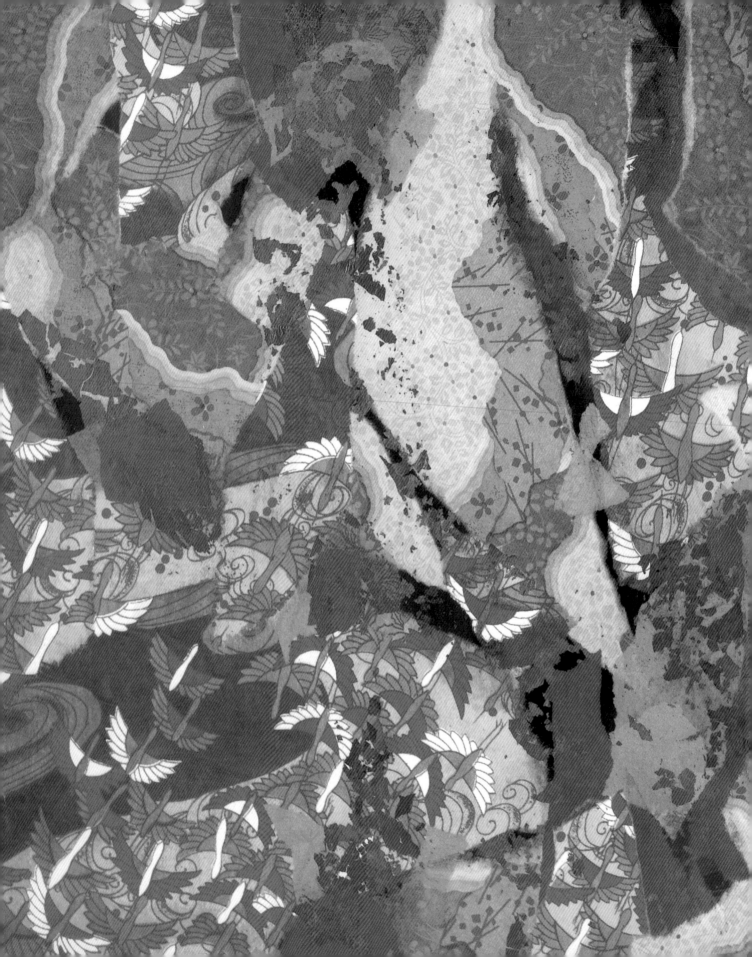

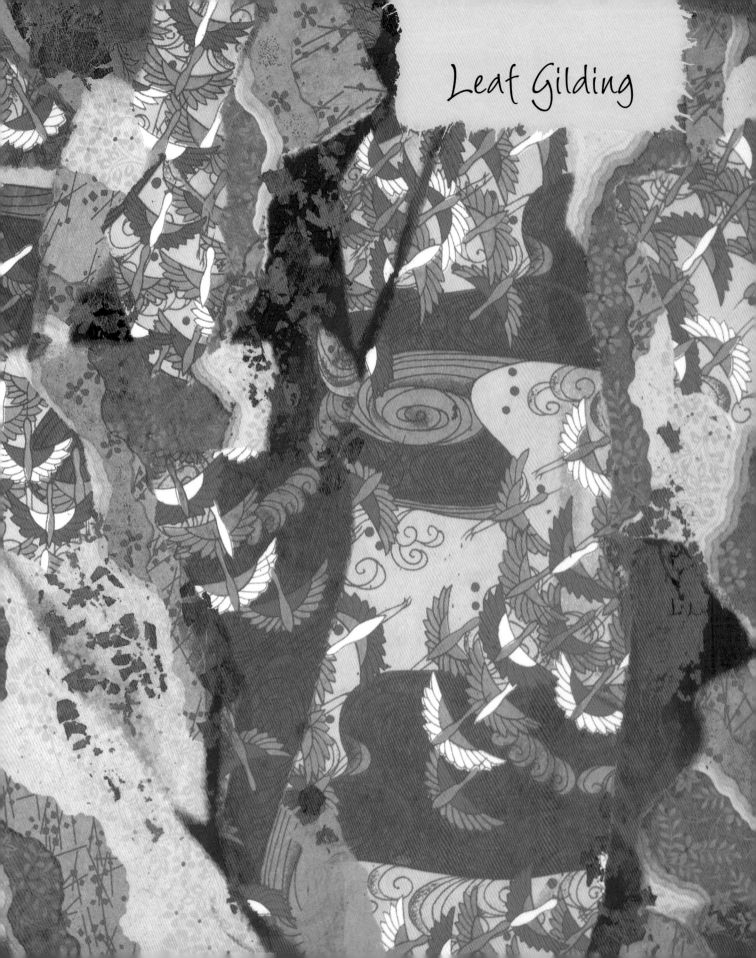

Leaf Gilding

Leaf Gilding

Materials
Acrylic paints: metallics of choice
Découpage medium
Japanese Yuzen Kimono paper:
  patterns and colors of choice
Leafing: gold; copper
Tissue paper: metallic gold

General Supplies & Tools
Paintbrushes: 1" flat watercolor (2)

Instructions
1. Refer to Preparing Surfaces on page 8. Prepare project surface.

2. Using a flat paintbrush, randomly brush metallic colors of paint onto project surface, gently blending colors. Let dry. Repeat process to create a saturated, jewel-like appearance.

3. Tear papers into random shapes and sizes suitable to project.

4. Using another flat paintbrush, apply découpage medium onto project surface, working small areas at a time. Press papers into medium, leaving bits of painted metallic areas exposed. Let dry. Repeat process until surface is covered as desired. Let dry.

5. Using a flat paintbrush, dry-brush small amount of découpage medium onto project surface. Pick up piece of leafing on finger and smear it into découpage medium (fig. 1). Let dry.

Repeat process until desired amount of leafing has been applied to surface.

6. Brush several coats of découpage medium over papered surface, allowing medium to dry between each coat.

Materials: Japanese Yuzen Kimono paper, acrylic paints, découpage medium, gold tissue paper, and gold and copper leafing.

(fig. 1) Working small areas at a time, dry-brush a small amount of découpage medium as desired onto project surface.

Antiqued Papers

Materials

Acrylic paints: metallics; additional colors of choice

Colored paper of choice: two shades with no pattern

Découpage medium

Japanese fiber paper, white: light- and medium-weight

Leaves: assorted

Tissue paper: metallic

General Supplies & Tools

Disposable paint palette

Hard plastic sheet: crushed-ice texture

Paintbrushes: 1" flat watercolor (2)

Small sponge

Spray bottle filled with water

Instructions

1. Refer to Preparing Surfaces on page 8. Prepare project surface.

2. Tear one colored paper into random shapes and sizes suitable to project. Tear medium-weight fiber paper into random shapes and sizes, slightly smaller than colored paper pieces.

3. Spray front and back of colored paper pieces with a light mist of water. Using a flat paintbrush, apply découpage medium onto project surface and press paper pieces into medium. Overlap and brush with more medium to seal edges. Let dry.

4. Brush another coat of découpage medium onto project surface and press fiber paper pieces into medium, leaving

areas of colored paper pieces exposed. Let dry.

5. Dilute 1–2 drops of each color of paint with one tablespoon water on palette. Using damp sponge, apply paints onto light-weight fiber paper to stain (fig. 1). Allow paints to mix and feather together. Let dry.

6. Using another flat paintbrush, dry-brush a light coat of full-strength color of paint onto leaf. With paint side down and using paper from Step 4 and metallic tissue paper, carefully press leaf onto pieces of paper to imprint. Repaint leaf and repeat process for desired number of leaves.

7. Dry-brush desired color of paint onto textured plastic (fig. 2). Stamp plastic pattern onto papered surface. Let dry.

8. Tear leaves from papers. Using a flat paintbrush, apply découpage medium over papered surface and gently press paper leaves into medium. Leaves may be crunched, pushed together, and edges overlapped to add texture.

9. Tear second colored paper into random shapes and sizes. Brush découpage medium over papered surface and press papers into medium. Let dry.

10. Using a sponge, paint entire surface with metallic color of paint. Let dry, then, using a flat paintbrush, apply several coats of découpage medium onto papered surface, allowing medium to dry between each coat.

Materials: Colored paper, Japanese fiber paper, metallic tissue paper, leaves, acrylic paints, and découpage medium.

(fig. 1) Sponge diluted paint onto lightweight paper to stain. Cover all white areas, allowing edges to feather and bleed into one another.

(fig. 2) Dry-brush desired colors onto "crushed-ice" texture plastic, creating a plate for printing a veined design on paper.

Antiqued Papers

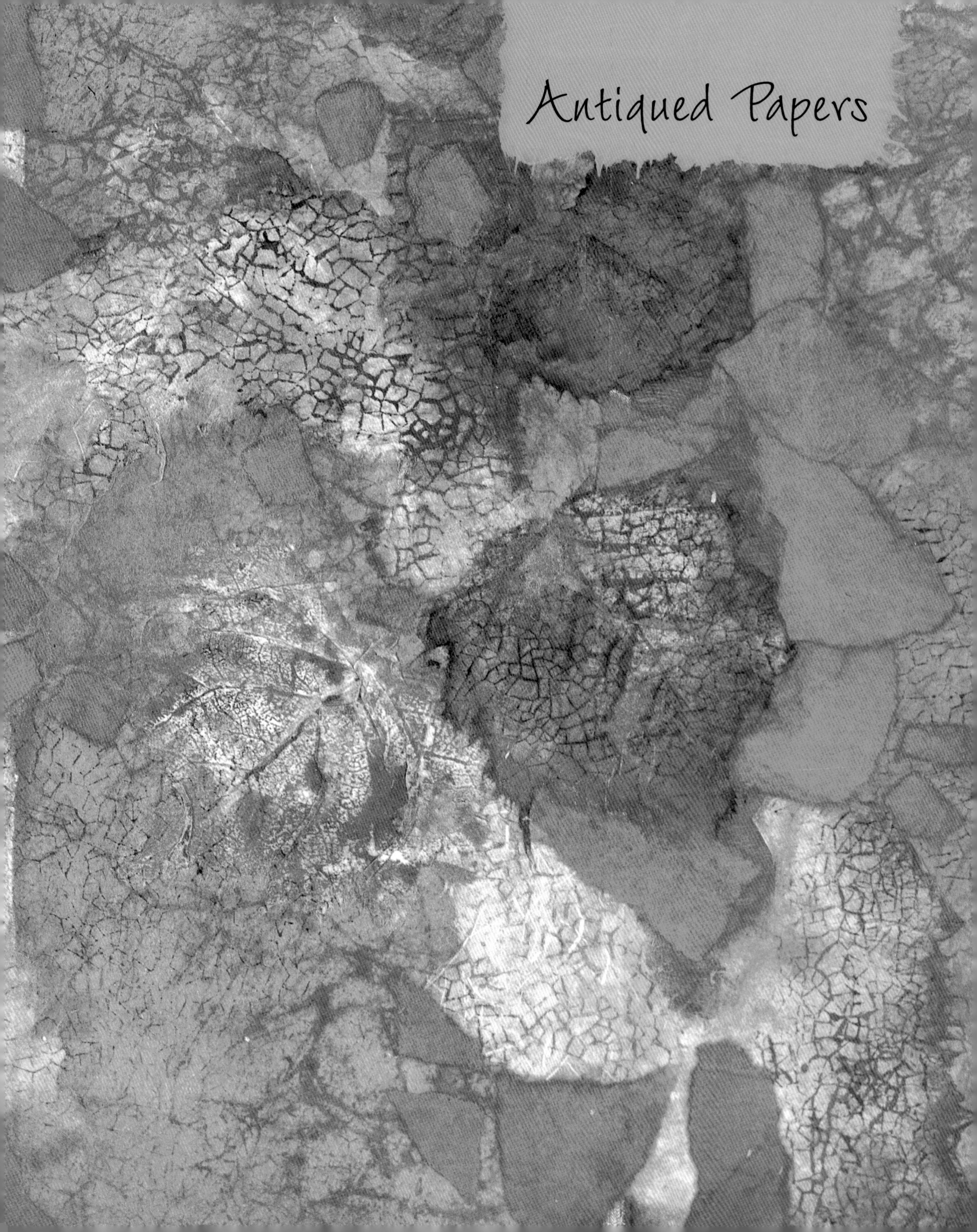

Reverse Découpage

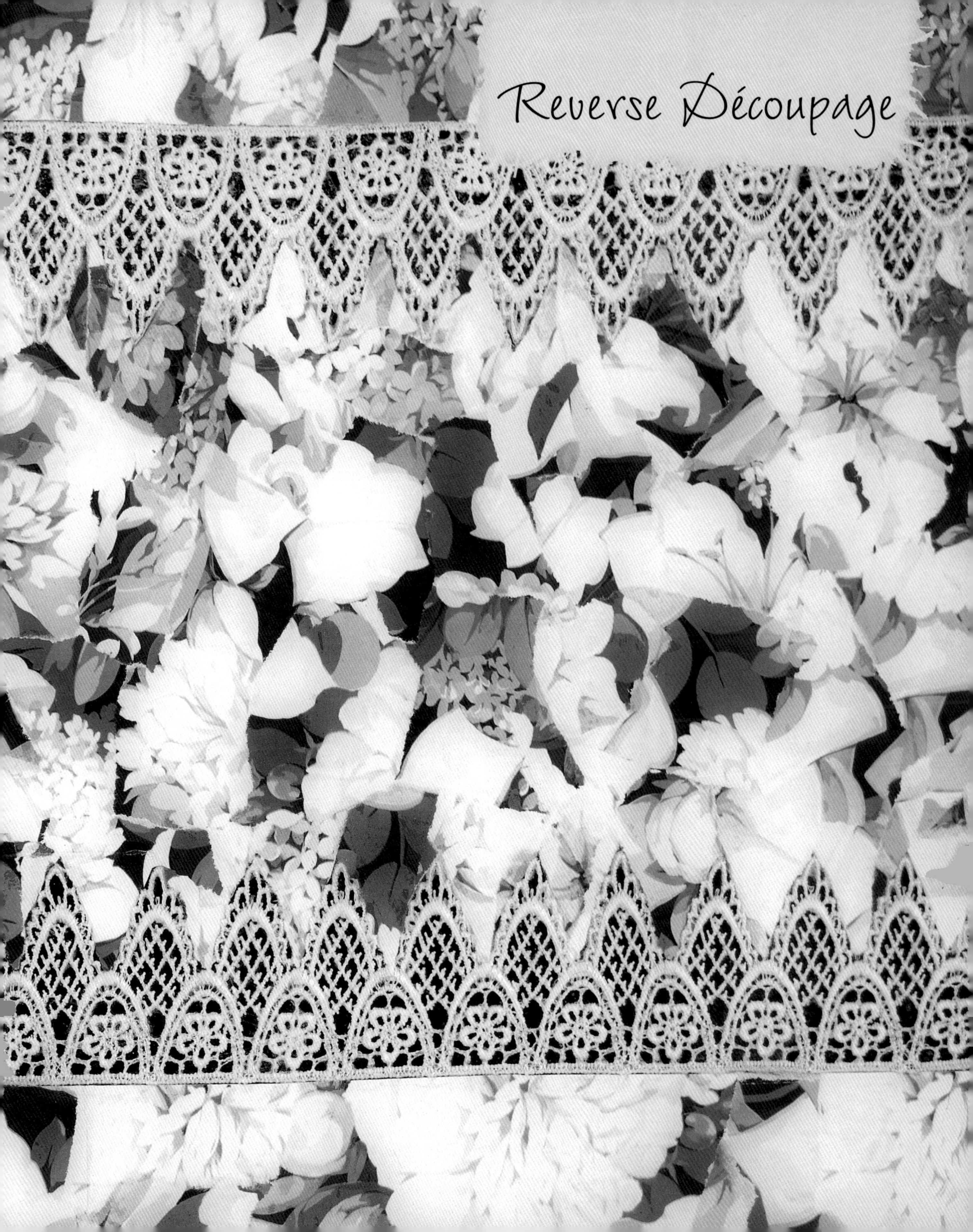

Reverse Découpage

Materials
Découpage medium
Glass object
Lace: 1½"-wide
Tissue paper: color or pattern of choice

General Supplies & Tools
Dishwashing soap
Fabric scissors
Paintbrushes: 1" flat watercolor

Instructions
NOTE: A glass project is always découpaged on the inside or backside of the surface.

1. Clean glass with soap and water. Dry thoroughly.

2. Cut lace to fit desired areas. Brush découpage medium onto desired areas and press lace into medium. Brush more medium over lace to seal.

3. Tear tissue paper into random shapes and sizes suitable to project, making certain all straight edges are torn. Brush découpage medium to project surface and press right sides of paper pieces into medium, slightly overlapping each piece (fig. 1). Do not apply papers to lace. Let dry.

4. Brush a final coat of découpage medium over entire project surface.

(fig. 1) Press right sides of torn tissue paper pieces onto surface that has been coated with découpage medium. Slightly overlap each paper piece.

Fleurage

Materials
Acrylic paints: metallic silver;
  additional colors of choice
Découpage medium
Dried flower blossoms and petals
Gift wrap: floral
Ribbons: 1½"-wide sheer organza;
  2½"-wide sheer embroidered metallic

General Supplies & Tools
Craft tip set: fine-point
Crewel needle: large
Disposable paint palette
Paintbrushes: 1" flat watercolor
Paper towels
Small sponge

Instructions
1. Refer to Preparing Surfaces on page 8. Prepare project surface.

2. Squeeze a small amount of each color of paint onto palette. Using a damp sponge, randomly apply color of paint onto surface. Rinse sponge clean and repeat process with each color until surface is covered.

3. Brush edges of gift wrap with clean water. Using crewel needle, pull at wet edges, creating a feathery edge. Let dry.

4. Brush découpage medium onto sponged surface. Press gift wrap into medium. Brush a coat of medium over gift wrap, gently smoothing wrinkles. Let dry.

5. Brush découpage medium onto gift wrap. Press ribbons into medium. Using fingers or a pad of paper towels, smooth ribbons. Let dry.

6. Brush découpage medium onto desired areas and gently place flower blossoms and petals into medium. Apply more medium to secure. Do not touch blossoms or petals with fingers or paper towels until they are dry.

7. Following manufacturer's instructions for use of craft tip set, outline desired areas with silver metallic paint. Let dry 1–2 hours.

8. Brush several coats of découpage medium over papered surface, allowing medium to dry between each coat.

Materials: Sheer organza and metallic ribbon, dried flower blossoms, acrylic paints, and découpage medium.

Fleurage

Harmony

Harmony

Materials
Acrylic paint: metallic gold
Découpage medium
Gift wrap: patterned
Japanese Momi paper
Leafing: gold; copper
Plastic acetate: .05 mil
Wild Fiber maché

General Supplies & Tools
Craft tip set: fine-point
Découpage scissors
Iron and ironing board
Paintbrushes: 1" flat watercolor
Rolling pin

Instructions

1. Refer to Preparing Surfaces on page 8. Prepare project surface.

2. Following manufacturer's instructions for making lace paper, mix maché and roll between sheets of plastic acetate (fig. 1). Let dry.

3. Carefully remove handmade lace paper from acetate. If necessary, paper may be flattened by pressing with an iron on medium/low heat (fig. 2).

4. Tear handmade lace paper and Momi paper into random shapes and sizes suitable for project.

5. Cut out designs from gift wrap.

6. Brush découpage medium onto project surface, working small areas at a time. Press Momi paper pieces into découpage medium and smooth with paintbrush. Brush a coat of découpage medium over papered surface. Let dry. Repeat process to adhere handmade lace paper pieces in desired areas. Adhere gift wrap designs.

7. Following manufacturer's instructions for use of craft tip set, outline desired areas with gold metallic color of paint. Let dry 1–2 hours.

8. Randomly brush découpage medium onto small areas of papered surface and apply gold and copper leafing. Let dry.

9. Brush 5–7 coats of découpage medium onto papered surface, allowing medium to dry between each coat.

Materials: Wild Fiber maché, découpage medium, rolling pin, and iron.

(fig. 1)   Roll mixed maché between sheets of plastic acetate.

(fig. 2)   Upon removing handmade lace paper from acetate, flatten by pressing with an iron set on medium/low heat.

Techniques 77

Tape Texture

Materials
Acrylic paints: lt. brown; additional
  color of choice
Découpage medium
Japanese Unryu paper: sheer white
Masking tape: ¾"-wide
Patterned ribbon

General Supplies & Tools
Craft sponge: shape of choice
Découpage scissors
Disposable paint palette
Paintbrushes: 1" flat watercolor
Paper towels
Small sponge

Instructions
1. Refer to Preparing Surfaces on page
8. Prepare project surface.

2. Tear masking tape into small random
shapes and sizes suitable to project.
Adhere tape to project surface in
desired pattern, overlapping straight
edge on tape with torn edge of another
piece of tape (fig. 1). When pattern is
complete, make certain all tape edges
are sealed.

3. Squeeze lt. brown color of paint onto
palette. Using damp sponge, apply
color in a circular motion onto taped
surface for a stained appearance (fig. 2).
If color is too dark, it may be removed
with a damp paper towel. Work only
small areas at a time.

4. Brush découpage medium over
taped surface. Let dry.

5. Squeeze a small amount of color of
paint color onto palette. Using craft
sponge, apply color onto desired areas
of taped surface. Let dry. Brush a coat
of découpage medium over project
surface.

6. Cut motifs from patterned ribbon.

7. Brush découpage medium onto
desired areas of project surface and
press ribbon motifs into medium. Let
dry.

8. Tear Unryu paper into random
shapes and sizes. Brush découpage
medium onto desired areas of surface
and press paper pieces into medium.
Paper pieces may be pushed to form
subtle wrinkles and overlapped for
added interest. Let dry.

9. Brush several coats of découpage
medium over papered surface, allowing
medium to dry between each coat.

(fig. 1) Adhere torn pieces of masking tape to project surface as desired, overlapping straight edge of tape with torn edge of another piece of tape.

(fig. 2) Using a small, damp sponge, apply paint in a circular motion onto taped surface for a stained appearance. Work small areas at a time.

Paper Lacquer

Paper Lacquer

Materials
Acrylic paints: assorted
Black-and-white line drawing: design
  of choice
Découpage medium
Embossing ink: clear
Embossing powder: gold
Japanese Mulberry paper
Watercolor paints: assorted

General Supplies & Tools
Craft scissors
Crewel needle: large
Embossing pen
Heat tool
Paintbrushes: 1" flat watercolor;
  #2 round; #8 round
Rubber stamps: designs of choice

Instructions
1. Refer to Preparing Surfaces on page 8. Prepare project surface.

2. Tear Mulberry paper into random shapes and sizes suitable to project.

3. Using flat paintbrush, brush paper pieces with water until surface glistens. Using #8 round paintbrush, touch paintbrush in watercolor paints, then touch onto wet surface. Paint will spread and feather (fig. 1). More color can be added in the same way as the surface begins to dry. The shape of the brush stroke will show more as the paper becomes drier. To lighten colors, add more water. Let dry. Throroughly wash paintbrush.

4. Using flat paintbrush, brush découpage medium onto project surface, working small areas at a time. Press paper pieces into medium, saving several pieces for following step. Let dry.

5. Stamp paper pieces from Step 4. Sprinkle with embossing powder. Tap excess powder onto piece of paper for reuse. Using heat tool and following manufacturer's instructions, set designs (fig. 2). Take care to avoid blistering of découpage medium. Using tip of #8 round paintbrush, wet area around embossed design. Using crewel needle, gently pull paper away from edges of embossed design to create a feathered edge.

6. Cut design from line drawing. Brush découpage medium onto desired area of project surface and press design into medium. Repeat process for stamped designs.

7. Outline edge and trace over all lines of design with embossing pen and ink. Sprinkle with embossing powder and, using heat tool, set design.

8. Using #2 round paintbrush, paint desired areas of embossed design with acrylic colors of paint. Let dry. Using flat paintbrush, apply a coat of découpage medium. Let dry. Repaint detail areas.

9. Lightly sprinkle embossing powder across project surface and heat as before.

10. Brush papered surface with a final coat of découpage medium.

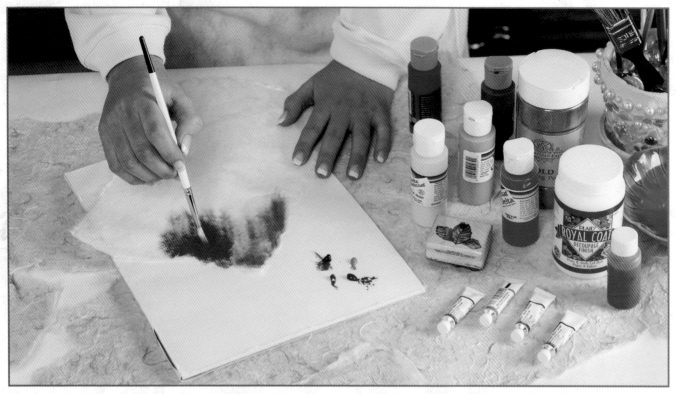

(fig. 1)   Using a round paintbrush, apply paint colors to wet paper, allowing edges to blend into each other.

(fig. 2)   Stamp design with embossing ink. Sprinkle embossing powder over design. Tap off excess powder and, using heat tool, emboss design.

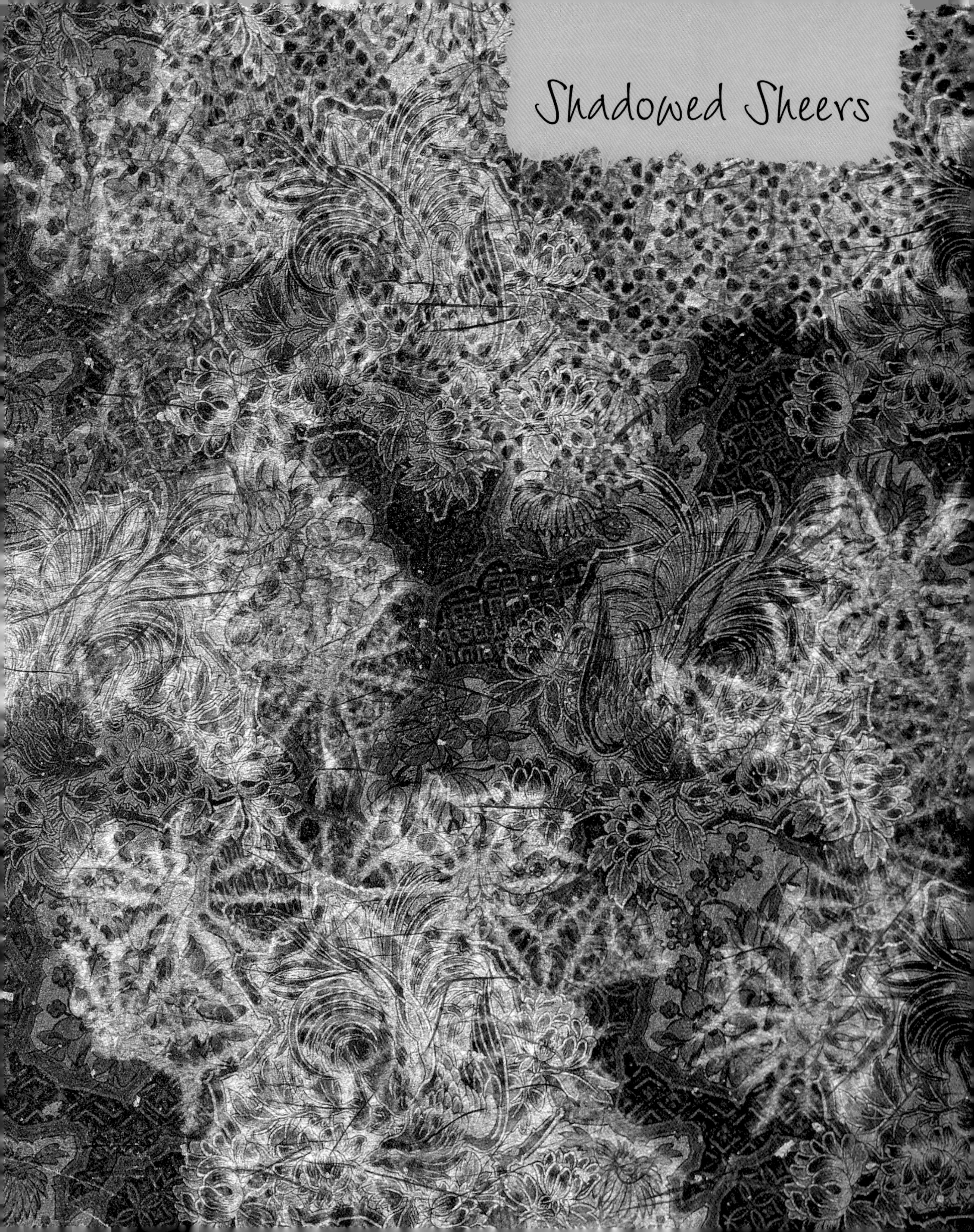
Shadowed Sheers

Shadowed Sheers

Instructions

1. Refer to Preparing Surfaces on page 8. Prepare project surface.

2. Brush découpage medium onto project surface. Working quickly, lay foil gift wrap in a "U" shape onto flat surface (fig. 1). Smooth with pad of paper towels, working from center to edge of foil. Using blow dryer set to low, dry.

3. Dilute one tablespoon découpage medium with two teaspoons water. Tear lace paper into random shapes and sizes suitable to project. Brush diluted medium over desired areas of foil gift wrap and adhere lace paper pieces. To smooth, rinse paintbrush and pat dry on paper towels, then gently brush from center to outside edges. Blow dry.

4. Brush diluted découpage medium over entire papered surface. Rinse paintbrush and pat dry on paper towels.

Lay Unryu paper over surface and gently brush to mesh paper layers. Blow dry.

5. Brush several coats of full-strength découpage medium over papered surface, allowing medium to dry between each coat.

Materials: Two different patterned Japanese lace papers, foil gift wrap, Japanese Unryu paper, and découpage medium.

(fig. 1) Working quickly, lay foil gift wrap in a "U" shape onto flat surface that has been coated with découpage medium. Smooth with paper towels from center to outside edges.

Trompe L'oeil

Materials
Découpage medium
Japanese Unryu paper: medium-weight
Marbleized paper
Poster of choice

General Supplies & Tools
Craft knife
Cutting surface: glass or cutting mat
Metal-edge ruler
Paintbrushes: 1" flat watercolor
Sewing needle: fine point
Small flat sponge

Instructions
1. Refer to Preparing Surfaces on page 8. Prepare project surface.

2. Using craft knife and ruler, cut image from poster in desired shape and size on cutting surface.

3. Brush generous coat of découpage medium onto project surface.

4. Position print and gently press into medium. Smooth print with damp sponge, working from center to outside edges. Poster print paper tends to bubble. Using needle, prick any remaining bubbles and work area until flat.

5. Brush découpage medium over print and let dry.

6. Tear papers into random shapes and sizes suitable to project.

7. Brush découpage medium onto areas surrounding print. Press papers into medium. Brush gently to flatten and blend edges.

8. Brush several coats of découpage medium over papered surface, allowing medium to dry between each coat.

Trompe L'oeil

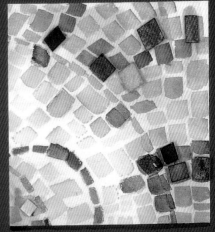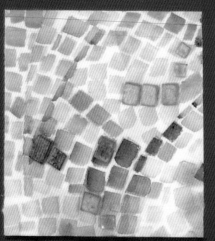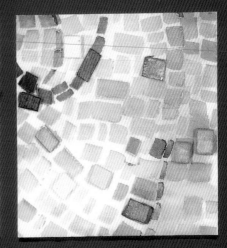

Paper Mosaic

Materials
Acrylic paints: colors of choice
Artwork with mosaic tile pattern
Découpage medium
Watercolor paper: 140 lb.

General Supplies & Tools
Aluminum foil
Craft knife with #11 blade
Craft scissors
Cutting surface: glass or cutting mat
Metal-edge ruler
Paintbrushes: 1" flat watercolor
Plastic cups
Small sponge

Instructions
1. Refer to Preparing Surfaces on page 8. Prepare project surface.

2. Using craft knife and ruler, cut watercolor paper into ¼"-wide strips on cutting surface.

3. For each color desired, mix one teaspoon paint with ¼ cup water in plastic cup, making certain paint is dissolved and no lumps remain.

4. Using scissors, cut paper strips into ¼" chips. Mix chips in paint cups. Soak chips for approximately one hour (fig. 1). Remove chips and place on aluminum foil to dry.

5. Cut artwork to fit project surface. Using sponge, dampen backside of artwork.

6. Brush découpage medium onto project surface. Press artwork into medium. Gently smooth to remove any bubbles. Let dry.

7. Brush découpage medium onto artwork surface. Randomly place chips in medium as desired. Let dry.

8. Brush several coats of découpage medium over project surface, allowing medium to dry between each coat.

(fig. 1) Soak paper chips in plastic cups filled with diluted paint. Remove chips when desired color is acheived.

Oriental Froissage

Materials
Acrylic paints: colors of choice
Butcher paper
Découpage medium
Patterned paper
Pearlized glaze

General Supplies & Tools
Découpage scissors
Disposable paint palette
Iron and ironing board
Paintbrushes: 1" flat watercolor (2)
Pressing cloth
Spray bottle filled with water

Instructions
1. Refer to Preparing Surfaces on page 8. Prepare project surface.

2. Crumple butcher paper into a tight wad, then open up and smooth on a flat, clean surface. Spray paper with water, then crumple up again. Open paper up and smooth flat, shiny side up.

3. Squeeze a small amount of each color paint onto palette. Re-spray paper surface. Using a flat paintbrush, dip in clean water, then pick up a paint color. Lightly brush paper, allowing color to bleed (fig. 1). Repeat process with each color, allowing colors to bleed and overlap as desired. Re-spray surface as needed.

4. Brush glaze over entire papered surface. When dry, cover surface with pressing cloth and press with hot iron.

5. Using another flat paintbrush, apply découpage medium onto project surface. Lay watercolored butcher paper over medium and gently smooth onto project surface. Brush 5–7 coats of découpage medium over papered surface, allowing medium to dry between each coat.

6. Cut out designs from patterned paper. Brush découpage medium onto desired areas of surface. Arrange and press designs into medium.

7. Brush several coats of découpage medium over papered surface, allowing medium to dry between each coat.

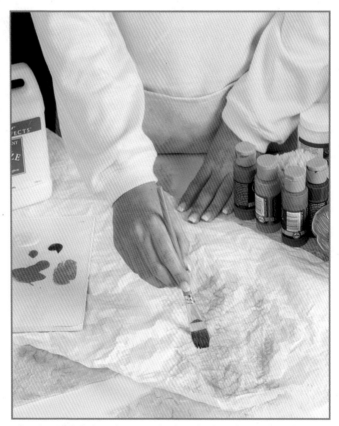

(fig. 1) Lightly brush crumpled and misted paper with paint, allowing colors to bleed into each other.

Oriental Froissage

Faux Smoked Paper

Faux Smoked Paper

Materials
Acrylic paints: assorted colors
Découpage medium
Embossing ink: clear
Embossing powder: metallic
Japanese Mulberry paper: white
Watercolor paper: white, 140 lb.,
  hot press (smooth)
Waterproof ultra-fine point marker:
  .01 tip

General Supplies & Tools
Blow dryer
Crewel needle: large
Disposable paint palette
Heat tool
Paintbrushes: 1" flat watercolor (2);
  #2 round watercolor
Rubber stamps: designs of choice
Spray bottle filled with water

Instructions
1. Refer to Preparing Surfaces on page 8. Prepare project surface.

2. Using flat paintbrush, lightly brush clean water onto watercolor paper until surface glistens.

3. For each color of paint, mix one part paint with five parts water on palette. Mix well.

4. Lightly brush darkest color of paint onto wet paper, working vertically top to bottom (fig. 1). If the color appears too intense or does not feather and bleed, rinse brush and apply more water to surface. Continue by adding colors across surface. Colors should be pale and very soft-edged. Blow dry.

5. Using spray bottle, mist edges of paper. Using round paintbrush, brush a diluted paint color toward center of paper (fig. 2). For more intense color, additional paint may be brushed on even as paper dries. Less water and more paint will make a stronger color. Repeat process several times to build deeper colors as desired. Blow dry.

6. Using marker and beginning at top left corner of page, randomly draw a meandering line across watercolored paper (fig. 3). Do not lift pen; draw a continuous, flowing line.

7. Ink stamp with embossing ink and stamp onto Mulberry paper. Sprinkle with embossing powder. Tap excess powder onto piece of paper for reuse. Using heat tool and following manufacturer's instructions, set design.

8. Using round paintbrush, paint areas of stamped image as desired. Rinse paintbrush, then dip in clean water and brush paper around outside edges of stamped designs. Using crewel needle, gently pull excess paper from edges, leaving a feathery edge. Lift shape. Blow dry.

9. Using another flat paintbrush, brush découpage medium onto desired areas of watercolored paper. Lay stamped designs in medium and gently press into medium. Let dry.

10. Keeping paper flat, lightly dust embossing powder across papered surface. Heat with heat tool.

11. Brush several coats of découpage medium over papered surface, allowing medium to dry between each coat.

(fig. 1) Vertically stroke paint colors across wet paper from top to bottom. Apply more water to increase feathering.

(fig. 2) After misting paper with spray bottle, pull colors toward center, building deeper color at outside edges.

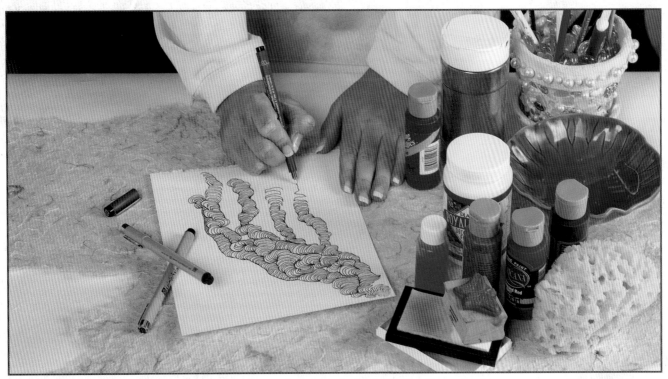

(fig. 3) Using non-bleeding, permanent fine-line marker, make "trails" by letting line meander across paper. The closer the line is drawn, the darker the trail. The further apart the line, the more feathered it appears.

Faux Tortoise Shell

Faux Tortoise Shell

Materials
Acrylic paints: assorted metallics
Antique map: colored copy
Art paper: assorted colors
Clip-art: trees; leaves (copy to desired
  size)
Découpage medium
Embossing ink: clear
Embossing powder: gold
Indian paper: gold stripe
Isopropyl alcohol
Tissue paper, metallic: gold; copper;
  black gold; gold and white striped

Supplies & Tools
Craft knife with #11 blade
Craft scissors
Cutting surface: glass or cutting mat
Heat tool
Masking tape
Paintbrushes: 1" flat watercolor (2);
  #2 script liner
Plastic cups
Rubber stamps: African prints; animal
  hide prints; giraffe hide; small leaf; vine

Instructions
1. Refer to Preparing Surfaces on page
8. Prepare project surface.

2. Using flat paintbrush, brush diluted découpage medium onto colored art paper. Let dry.

3. Dilute desired metallic color with clean water in plastic cup until of a thin, ink-like consistancy. Mix well. Pour 2 ounces alcohol into another cup.

4. Using another flat paintbrush, brush diluted metallic paint uniformly onto art paper. Before wash dries, and using liner paintbrush, touch droplets of alcohol onto surface of wet paint (fig. 1). Paint will push away from tip of paintbrush into irregular circles. Continue as desired. Let dry.

5. Tear antique map from color copy.

6. Tear striped tissue, Indian paper, and metallic tissue into random shapes and sizes.

7. Ink stamps with embossing ink and stamp onto colored metallic tissue. Sprinkle with embossing powder. Tap excess powder onto piece of paper for reuse. Using heat tool and following manufacturer's instructions, set designs. Tear images from tissue.

8. Using small pieces of masking tape, tape clip-art to painted art paper. Place on cutting surface. Using craft knife, cut through pattern and art paper for finished motifs. Using scissors, trim and clean motifs.

9. Using flat paintbrush, brush medium onto area where map is to be adhered. Press map into medium and brush gently to remove bubbles. Adhere other torn paper pieces.

10. Repeat Step 9, adhering motifs. Brush several coats of decoupage medium over papered surfaces, allowing medium to dry between each coat.

Materials: Isopropyl alcohol, colored art paper, acrylic paints, découpage medium.

(fig. 1)   Touch droplets of alcohol onto surface of wet paint that has been washed onto colored art paper. The alcohol will cause rings to form in the paint, producing a subtle tortoise shell effect.

Fabrics & Fibers

Fabrics & Fibers

Materials
Découpage medium
Fabric: assorted patterns and colors
Faceted-head upholstery tacks
Gift wrap: patterned with fabric
   appearance
Ribbons: assorted widths, colors, and
   textures
Tissue paper: printed texture

General Supplies & Tools
Paintbrushes: 1" watercolor
Scissors: craft; fabric
Small hammer

Instructions
1. Refer to Preparing Surfaces on page 8. Prepare project surface.

2. Using craft scissors, cut gift wrap and tissue paper into squares and rectangles suitable in size to project. Using fabric scissors, cut fabric and ribbon into squares and rectangles.

3. Brush découpage medium onto project surface, working small areas at a time. Press tissue paper into medium. Gently brush to flatten. Continue, layering fabric, paper, and ribbon, until desired look is achieved (fig. 1). Let dry.

4. Hammer upholstery tacks into project surface as desired.

5. Brush several coats of découpage medium over papered surface and tacks, allowing medium to dry between each coat.

Materials: Patterned gift wrap, patterned fabric, ribbons, and découpage medium.

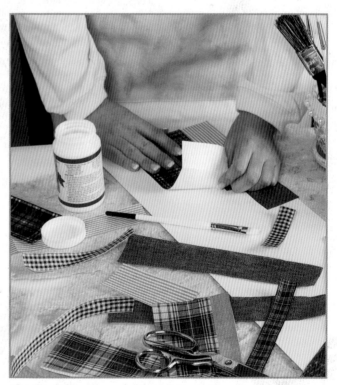

(fig. 1) Press strips of ribbon into decoupage medium. Place paper strips adjacent to ribbon, carefully butting edges together for a clean appearance.

The photographs on the following pages are provided to show "practical application" of some of the previous faux-page techniques for personalizing home decor items.

Victorian Candy Jar

Lace and decorative paper combine to create an eye-catching and functional container. The reverse method enhances the shape of the glass. Refer to *Reverse Découpage* technique on pages 68 and 70.

Candleholders faux Natural

A surface as difficult as concrete (these candleholders *are* made of concrete) can be transformed into something lovely, by the application of faux painting techniques, interesting papers, and natural preserved leaves acquired from a local craft or floral store. Refer to *Foliage* technique on pages 24–25 and 26.

Letter & Cache Box

Feathery tissue papers can be layered to create many effects. Here, the solid look of marble diguises an ordinary wooden box. Foreign post cards and postage stamps set the theme for its use. Refer to *Faux Marble* technique on pages 28 and 30.

Ginger Jar Lamp

A plain ceramic lamp base and plastic shade become an exquisite accessory when covered with a pearl-glazed paper and old fashioned roses cut from gift wrap. Refer to *Glazing Paper* technique on pages 34 and 36.

Child's Contempo Chair

A lighthearted effect is acheived on this worn, but well-loved, child's chair by giving it a fresh coat of paint and adding just a few stickers and motifs cut from decorative stationery. Refer to *Bits & Pieces* technique on pages 46 and 48–49.

Brown Paper Chic

Fast, easy, and inexpensive too, this technique, using heavy brown paper, can cover a multitude of flaws that are the result of years of wear and tear. Refer to *Faux Leather* technique on pages 54 and 56.

Starflight Table

The color and texture found on pages gleaned from ordinary magazines yeild various themes, including the popular celestial blues and golds. Refer to *Pictures for Design* technique on pages 57 and 58.

Gilded Chairs

Rich and exotic looking, it is hard to believe that the surface on these chairs is created with only a few layers of paint and torn papers. Refer to *Leaf Gilding* technique on pages 60 and 62–63.

Textured Hutch

A unique artistic touch is given to an assembly line piece of furniture. Colors and textures can be personalized to complement an existing decor. The faux terra-cotta in this piece is actually a recycled colored file folder that was torn into pieces. Refer to *Antiqued Papers* technique on pages 63–65 and 66.

Memory Box

Roses for remembrance. Add a contemporary touch to a box designed for holding precious photographs. The gold outline of the floral design is reflective of those memories that even time won't dim. Refer to *Papier Appliqué* technique on pages 16 and 18–19.

Curio Shelf

Flower petals saved from a special garden lend romance to a shelf for displaying small momentos. Special occasion ribbons add to the nostalgia. Refer to *Fleurage* technique on pages 71 and 72.

Magazine Rack

An out of date throw-away was transformed into a pleasing and functional accessory to the reading room. Handmade lace paper and gold outlining add intrigue to this easy, but unusual project. Refer to *Harmony* technique on pages 74 and 76–77.

Ivy Birdhouse

Masking tape does more than simply hold things together. Small overlapping pieces of tape define scale and provide an understated texture. Refer to *Tape Texture* technique on pages 78 and 80–81.

Gossamer Mirror

Layering tissue sheers over foil gift wrap gives the illusion of softness and depth to a hard, flat surface. Refer to *Shadowed Sheers* technique on pages 86 and 88–89.

Exotic Tea Service

An old technique, mosaic, using new materials and bold colors, brightens a decorative tray. To make the piece functional and durable, the design is set in resin. Refer to *Paper Mosaic* technique on pages 92 and 94.

Oriental Chest

This chest was given new life by applying crinkled butcher paper over its entire surface. Motifs cut from wall paper enhance the subtle shading in the textured paper. Refer to *Oriental Froissage* technique on pages 95 and 96.

Butterfly Mirror

Lacy butterflies and soft watercolor washes are applied to small inset areas of this ornate mirror. Refer to *Faux Smoked Paper* technique on pages 98 and 100–101.

Denim Nightstand

Ribbons, fabric, and paper combine for a comtemporary country patchwork on this small chest of drawers. Decorative upholstery tacks and metal buttons complete the theme. Refer to *Fabrics & Fibers* technique on pages 106 and 108.

Product Suppliers

Plaid Enterprises Inc.
P.O. Box 7600
Norcross, Georgia 30091-7600
phone: (800) 842-4197
  acrylic paints and Royal Coat
  découpage medium

DecoArts Americana Paint
P.O. Box 386
Stanford, Kentucky 40484
phone: (606) 365-3193
  acrylic paints

Delta Technical Coatings
2550 Pellisier Place
Whittier, California 90601
distributed: arts and crafts stores
  nationwide
  acrylic paints, glazes, and crackle
  medium

Havel Scissors
3726 Lousdale Street
Cincinnati, Ohio 45227
phone: (800) 638-4770
  découpage scissors

Fiskars
P.O. Box 8027
Wausau, Wisconsin 54402-8027
phone: (715) 842-2091
  craft and fabric scissors

New Basics
P.O. Box 1739
Arvada, Colorado 80001-1739
phone: (800) 944-8981
  Wild Fiber papier maché

Daniel Smith
4150 First Avenue South
P.O. Box 84268
Seattle, Washington 98124-5568
phone: (800) 426-6740
fax: (800) 238-4065
catalog: $5.00
  exotic papers

New York Central Art Supply, Inc.
62 Third Avenue
New York, New York 10013
phone: (800) 950-6111
fax: (212) 475-2513
  exotic papers

Aiko's Art Materials
3347 N. Clark Street
Chicago, Illinois 60657
phone: (773) 404-5600
  exotic papers

Ichiyo Art Center
432 East Paces Ferry Road
Atlanta, Georgia 30305
phone: (800) 535-2263
fax: (404) 233-8012
catalog: $25.00
  exotic papers

Metric Equivalency Chart

mm-millimetres   cm-centimetres
inches to millimetres and centimetres

inches	mm	cm	inches	cm	inches	cm
⅛	3	0.3	9	22.9	30	76.2
¼	6	0.6	10	25.4	31	78.7
½	13	1.3	12	30.5	33	83.8
⅝	16	1.6	13	33.0	34	86.4
¾	19	1.9	14	35.6	35	88.9
⅞	22	2.2	15	38.1	36	91.4
1	25	2.5	16	40.6	37	94.0
1¼	32	3.2	17	43.2	38	96.5
1½	38	3.8	18	45.7	39	99.1
1¾	44	4.4	19	48.3	40	101.6
2	51	5.1	20	50.8	41	104.1
2½	64	6.4	21	53.3	42	106.7
3	76	7.6	22	55.9	43	109.2
3½	89	8.9	23	58.4	44	111.8
4	102	10.2	24	61.0	45	114.3
4½	114	11.4	25	63.5	46	116.8
5	127	12.7	26	66.0	47	119.4
6	152	15.2	27	68.6	48	121.9
7	178	17.8	28	71.1	49	124.5
8	203	20.3	29	73.7	50	127.0

Index